EVOLUTIONARY SOCIALISM

EDUARD BERNSTEIN

EVOLUTIONARY SOCIALISM

A Criticism and Affirmation

INTRODUCTION BY SIDNEY HOOK

SCHOCKEN BOOKS · NEW YORK

*Die Voraussetzungen des Sozialismus und die Aufgaben
der Sozialdemokratie*
Translated by Edith C. Harvey

First SCHOCKEN PAPERBACK Edition 1961

Fifth Printing, 1970

Library of Congress Catalog Card No. 61-16649
Manufactured in the United States of America

CONTENTS

INTRODUCTION

EDUARD Bernstein is the father of socialist "revisionism." The term "revisionism," however, is almost as
ambiguous as the term "socialism." Particularly today,
when the political ties of the communist world are
being fractured by charges of "revisionism," it
becomes necessary to distinguish the various movements and families of doctrine which are encompassed
by the name.

Bernstein's "revisionism" was a strong current in
the pre-World War I socialist movement. Latter-day
"revisionism" is a series of turbulent eddies in con-
temporary communism. Both have their source in
Marxism. Before expatiating on their differences,
something should be said about this common origin.
It speaks worlds about the nature of Marxism as a
movement and body of doctrine that the term
"revisionism" should be so largely employed in
Marxist circles as an epithet of abuse. Indeed, its
connotations of disparagement, deviation, incipient
betrayal, and apostasy are the only common elements
one can find in the wide variety of meanings the term
has in the literature of Marxism. In Marxist circles
to pin the label of "revisionist" on the ideas of a
socialist thinker is comparable to exposing a Christian
writer as a "heretic" or "atheist" during the heyday
of Western religious faith.

It was characteristic of Eduard Bernstein that he
frankly called himself a "revisionist." Without renouncing his allegiance to the socialist movement

and its ideals, he pointed to those developments in history and economics which invalidated some of Marx's analyses and predictions. He thus made the revision of Marx an intellectual necessity for those who wanted their scientific professions to square with experience. Unfortunately, they were not as numerous as Bernstein had expected. The reaction of "the true believers" to Bernstein's criticisms and the venomous nature of their attack upon him indicates that Bernstein was somewhat naive about the nature of mass movements. His position was rendered more uncomfortable by the fact that his criticisms of orthodox Marxism were highly praised in quarters that were hostile to all varieties of socialism. But Bernstein's intellectual courage measured up to his intellectual honesty. He stood his ground despite official condemnation of his criticisms and excited calls for his exclusion from the German Social Democratic Party. He restated and defended his position, never denying that he was a revisionist even when he protested against the misunderstandings of his revisionist views and the erroneous implications drawn from them by friend and foe.

After Bernstein—and probably because of the intensity of the anti-Bernstein jeremiad—none of the bold reinterpreters of Marx's work, whether they read Kant into his social thought or Blanqui into his theory of revolution, proclaimed themselves "revisionists." They repudiated suggestions that they were revising or modifying Marx's views. They insisted that they were merely restoring his thought, purifying it of its corruptions, and presenting it in its pristine form. The process of revising Marx by rediscovering him still continues. One modern expositor finds in Marx an anticipation of Freud; another that he is really a Zen-Buddhist, perhaps more accurately a Zen-Judaist. It may not be long before voices among the cultural *avant-garde* proclaim—on the basis of Marx's early writings, repudiated in his maturity—that what Marx really meant by his doctrine of "alienation" is what Kierkegaard and Heidegger have darkly expressed in the scriptural writings of existentialism.

What makes this hostility to the term "revisionism," and to the processes of critical examination of the cluster of ideas associated with Marxism, all the more paradoxical is the fierce insistence by those who regard themselves as the watchdogs of orthodoxy upon the "scientific" character of Marxism. For the very nature of a scientific statement requires that it be held tentatively, subject to the self-corrective procedures of the methods by which it is confirmed. One would have thought that to be scientific is to be committed to an attitude of revisionism. Bernstein himself never lost an opportunity to remind his critics that Marx and Engels had been the chief revisionists of the socialist thought of their day. Ever since Charles Peirce developed his theory of "critical fallibilism" in the latter half of the 19th century, it has become a commonplace that, in principle, every scientific statement can be challenged and withdrawn in the light of the evidence and in the interests of the systematic simplicity and fruitfulness of the body of knowledge of which it is a part. But to most socialists science was merely a set of doctrines which substituted for religion as a support of moral faith.

Bernstein was no revisionist in the sense in which

most men and movements have recently been labelled revisionist in Communist satellite countries. For he was primarily concerned with the *truth* of Marxism, while the latter, in order to avoid declaring Marx's judgments false, have sought to reconstruct his *meaning*. They have done this to some extent out of a misguided piety, to make Marx's thought immune to the refutation of events, but mainly to combat, in the name of Marxism, the absurd notions and abominable practices of the Communist regimes imposed on them under the banner of Marxism.

Nor has Bernstein's revisionism anything to do with the charges of revisionism hurled by the Chinese Communists against Tito and Khrushchev. The latter involves a struggle for the mantle of Lenin who was in important ways a more radical revisionist of Marx than was Bernstein. Lenin believed that the inevitable triumph of Communism on a world scale would be ushered in by inevitable war. Khrushchev, finally convinced that war with nuclear weapons might destroy both Communism and the free world, has proclaimed that the victory of Communism is still inevitable but not necessarily by inevitable war. He also believes that Communists may come to power in democratic countries by infiltration and guile, as in Czechoslovakia, rather than by armed insurrection. For these and allied reasons the Chinese Communists now regard Khrushchev as a "revisionist."

II

Eduard Bernstein was born in Berlin on January 6, 1850 into a family of modest means. His formal education was limited. At the age of sixteen he began his apprenticeship in a bank. A few years later he became a bank clerk, a post which he retained until he left Germany for Switzerland in 1878. Six years before that he had joined the Eisenacher socialist group which merged with the Lassallean socialist group in 1875 to form the German Social Democratic Party. In Switzerland, where Bernstein remained in consequence of Bismarck's anti-Socialist Laws, he edited the official Party newspaper. It was distributed clandestinely in Germany. In 1888, under pressure from Bismarck, Bernstein and the newspaper he edited were banished by the Swiss government. He then moved to London where he worked closely with Friedrich Engels, the collaborator of Marx. Indeed both Marx and Engels had thought highly of his editorial talents. Upon Engels' death, it was discovered that he had named Bernstein an executor of his estate and, together with Kautsky, his literary executor.*

Eduard Bernstein first presented some of his revisionist ideas in a series of articles on the problems of socialism in *Die Neue Zeit,* an official periodical. They precipitated a succession of political squalls in the German Social Democratic Party. To clarify and defend his position, Bernstein was induced to write the present work whose title, rendered literally, is *The Presuppositions of Socialism and the Tasks of Social Democracy.* Its publication transformed what had been mere squalls into a major political storm in both the German party and other European socialist parties—a storm which blew itself out only with the advent of the First World War.

---

* The best study in English of Bernstein's life and work is Peter Gay's The *Dilemma of Democratic Socialism,* Columbia University Press, New York, 1952.

Three things account for the startling, and to the orthodox, terrifying impact of Bernstein's book. First, it broke sharply with the apocalyptic conception that capitalism would collapse by virtue of inherent economic tendencies which would cause such widespread misery among the working classes that they would rise in revolutionary wrath, destroy the existing state, and introduce collective ownership of all major means of production, distribution, and exchange. Bernstein argued that the economic tendencies, upon which Marx predicated the collapse of capitalism, had not been fulfilled. The poor were not becoming poorer and the rich, richer. The doctrines of the increasing misery of the working class, the constant growth in size of the mass army of unemployed, the uninterrupted development of monopolies defying all social regulation, were not established by the facts. On the contrary, history had falsified them. Bernstein's explanation for the failure of Marx's predictions to materialize is that Marx had underestimated the economic and social consequences of the operation of a free political system upon its mode of production.

Secondly, Bernstein conceived of socialism as the fulfillment of the theory and practice of democracy in all social relations, the abolition of all class privileges, and the elimination of arbitrariness and unreasonable discrimination and inequality in human relationships. This meant that socialism must eschew any form of political dictatorship in the name of class or party. It also meant that the Socialist parties of the world, although their active membership would largely be drawn from the ranks of workers, must regard themselves as representing the *human* interest or the interests of *all* groups in society. Socialists must seek to establish not a proletarian society in place of a bourgeois society, but a society of universal citizenship. To do this, it would be necessary to take certain broad measures to socialize industry and to frustrate the will of those who seek to use their proprietorship as a means of lording it over men. Limits must also be set on certain kinds of freedom, like that of testamentary disposition, in order to permit greater freedom for the development of the individual. In the process of carrying out all these reforms, strict allegiance to legal, moderate, and constitutional methods of change must be observed. So conceived, democracy is not merely "government by the people" or "rule of the majority." The idea of democracy must include respect for minority rights, a notion of justice as well as human welfare. Spelled out, the demand for justice implies "an equality of rights for all members of the community, and in that principle the rule of the majority, to which in every concrete case the rule of the people extends, finds its limits."

Thirdly, the socialist movement must, in the formulation of its program, purge itself of the remaining elements of Utopianism. It must stop conceiving of itself as fulfilling "a final goal," and constantly realize itself in the myriad daily tasks, small or large, which confront the movement towards greater democratization. Whatever the ends of socialism, the means to achieve them must be continuous with these ends. This interrelatedness of means and ends requires no belief in a predetermined goal to guide it, but only a sense of the direction in which the socialist movement is going. The sentence which infuriated

Bernstein's socialist colleagues most was the one in which he declared that the socialist *movement* meant everything to him and what was usually called the *final aim* of socialism, nothing. Unfortunately phrased, it made it easy for hostile critics to charge that without reference to the aims or ideals of socialism one could not intelligently judge the direction of the movement. What Bernstein meant by his indifference to the final aim of socialism was not to its ideals but to the eloquent descriptions of the institutional forms of those ideals which no one at the time could really know.

In taking these positions Bernstein was doing little more than describing and approving the actual behavior, as distinct from the programmatic declarations, of the German Social Democratic movement and other Western socialist parties. But in demythologizing the socialist outlook, in pointing to the disparities between its holiday rhetoric and daily practice, in calling for greater empirical sobriety and less terminological pieties, Bernstein was criticizing not only the trappings of faith but its substance as well. He seemed unaware that the more effectively reformist the Social Democratic Party was, the more important for its members was the ideology of apocalypse and the hope for total solutions.

Nonetheless, the German Social Democratic Party before the First World War—and despite the shadow of excommunication poised over Bernstein's head—continued along the revisionist path. When the War broke out Bernstein himself wished the Party to take a firm stand against approval of the war budget. After the War his prestige soared and, until Hitler destroyed political democracy in Germany, his point of view, even doctrinally, was acceptable to the German Social Democratic Party. The presence of a Communist movement, completely controlled by the Soviet Union, facilitated the triumph of Bernstein's perspective. After the downfall of Hitler, when the German Social Democratic Party was reconstituted, Bernstein's ideas became the reigning orthodoxy. Perhaps he would have found them even too revisionist on strictly economic matters.

The organization of the Communist International at the close of the First World War drew off from the socialist movement the most dogmatic of the Marxists. Under the leadership of Lenin, the Communists revised Marxism so radically that in effect Marxism became a voluntaristic social philosophy which rationalized the seizure of political power anywhere on the globe. Through the dictatorship of the Communist Party, which was identified with the dictatorship of the proletariat, (even in countries in which the proletariat was of minuscular size), the Communists attempted by ruthless use of force to lay the economic foundations of socialism. Bernstein himself had been critical of the simplistic interpretation of the Marxist theory of historical materialism. He denied that economic forces uniquely determined politics and culture, and stressed the importance of ethical ideals and factors as well as the clash of economic interests in history. On some issues he was prepared to move more vigorously than his Social Democratic comrades who relied upon the working out of the underlying forces of history. But he saw in Bolshevik-Leninism, the theoretical foundation of Soviet Communism, a reversion to the extreme ideas of Blanqui and Bakunin which glorified force and violence under misleading formulas about historical necessity and the laws of the class struggle. When I saw him in 1929, a few years before his death in 1932, he was full of indignation over Communist immoralism, both in the Soviet Union and without. In speaking of his early years he added, with a touch of reminiscent asperity, that Marx had a Bolshevik streak in him apparent in his political relations to others. Bernstein insisted that with respect to doctrine, especially in its orientation towards democracy, cultural and intellectual freedom, Bolshevik-Leninism was little more than Asiatic despotism in modern dress.

If one examines the heritage of Bernstein, it seems fair to say that it is his ideas rather than those of his orthodox critics, Karl Kautsky and George Plekhanov, which have won the day, in the sense that they are reflected in the working beliefs of democratic socialist movements in the Western world. This is evidenced in various ways. First, democratic socialists today are aware that socialism and capitalism as systems of economy are neither exhaustive of all possibilities nor exclusive of each other. Few socialists believe in the collectivization of *all* means of production. They are aware that there is a totalitarian potential in a completely collectivized economy which, if political democracy is ever lost, may become a tremendous engine of oppression and tyranny. Secondly, they deny therefore that the chief issue of our time is between socialism and capitalism, a rationally controlled versus a free enterprise economy. Rather the struggle is between democracy, on the one hand, conceived not only politically but as a way of life, and totalitarianism on the other. The experience of Fascism and Communism has taught socialists, or reinforced what they once knew, that *freedom comes first*—the freedom to choose the economy, the religion, the cultural and artistic forms of existence under which one prefers to live. Instead of interpreting democracy merely as a means of achieving socialism, and therefore abandoning democracy, when it is slow or inefficient, for direct action or dictatorship or benevolent despotism, socialism becomes the institutional means by which the values of democracy are furthered. Thirdly, this implies that the socialist economy or the mode of production is not an end in itself, but is to be regarded as a means to a more abundant and a more just life. It then becomes an empirical matter, and not one of doctrinaire first principles, whether or not private ownership or public ownership or public corporate ownership—consisting of management, labor and consumers—is desirable in this or that particular sector of the economy. Fourthly, and perhaps most important, individual *persons* (not, of course, individualism as a theory) move into the forefront of concern in socialist philosophy. If, as Marx put it, "the free development of all (should) become the condition for the free development of each," then the ethical ideals of socialism are reinstated as the criteria for judging all existing institutions and all proposals for change. The content of morality goes beyond a set of abstract, categorical imperatives which cannot be applied to specific situations, even when they enjoy universal acceptance. It derives from the study of man in this particular time and society, of the alternatives of development open to him, their probable consequences, and reflective choice among them. This choice is guided by the ideals of equality or justice, joy or human welfare, and justified, to the extent that moral judgment can be justified, by intelligence. Although Bernstein spoke in another idiom — and few democratic socialists today are aware of the nature of the intellectual debt they owe him—by shattering the monolith of Marxist doctrinal orthodoxy, he prepared the way for the pluralism, the personalism, the orientation towards democracy as a way of life to which they are presently committed.

The democratic socialism for which Bernstein stood was not a milk and water doctrine of accommodation or adjustment to regnant power. Personally, Bernstein was fearless, both in following a sound argument no matter where it led and in struggling against aggression and injustice. In contradistinction to his early teachers and their disciples, he was fair to a fault in considering the views of others, including those of his critics. What is true of his personal character is true of his doctrine. He believed in vigorous action against those whose practices were hostile to democratic society, under no matter what colors they sailed. He did not fear far-reaching parliamentary reform and would personally have been willing to support stronger measures than those urged by the German Social Democrats after the First World War. In international affairs he was freer of chauvinism than most of his colleagues. He became, and remained, a good European from the very first days of his conversion to socialism. In the teeth of opposition from his own party, he laid the main burden of guilt for World War I at the door of Imperial Germany—

which reflected his moral passion against the official propaganda more than it did the actual weight of the evidence.

It is sometimes said of Bernstein's democratic socialism that it is viable only in a country already persuaded of the validity of his democratic ideals; that it is bankrupt when faced by the existence of such demonic social elements as those which cluster around men like Hitler or Lenin. This is a half truth. Bernstein would have agreed that democratic socialism could only be introduced into a country which believes in democracy. If a country does not believe in democracy, the conditions for socialism are unripe. The task of socialists in such a situation is to work to introduce the conditions under which democracy *can* develop, and to carry on intense educational activity on behalf of socialism. Bernstein regarded the Communists as unfaithful to the elementary principles of Marxism, as well as contemptuous of moral decency, because of their willingness to make a bloody sacrifice of living generations for a problematic future. For him the means determine the end more surely than the end determines the means. What results tomorrow is always the consequence of the means used today—and there is no empirical warrant for believing that a dictatorship based on lying propaganda and "force without limit," to use Lenin's expression, will eventuate in the brotherhood of man.

Bernstein would have repudiated—as a preface to, or apologia for, a political dictatorship—the recent declaration of a self-styled "socialist" leader of an African state that "it is an illusion to think you can have a revolution without prisons." This is not because Bernstein was a pacifist or opposed to the use of force, but because declarations of this kind are usually employed to justify repressive measures against democrats who think differently from the revolutionary junta in power. However, were a revolution initiated or established by the normal processes of democracy, Bernstein would not have hesitated to use force against active counter-revolutionists, Fascist or Communist. Judging by the principles he expressed, his first instincts would have been to introduce those measures of social reform which would remove legitimate grievances and therewith dissolve the mass base of totalitarian support. But he would not have hesitated to destroy a Hitler *before* Hitler succeeded in bringing down the whole structure of democracy into ruins. An impassioned believer in civil rights, Bernstein was not a ritualistic liberal, unable to distinguish between the heresy which a free society must tolerate and the conspiracy which it may not.

Eduard Bernstein has not yet come into his own. It is not hazardous, however, to predict that in those regions of the world which remain free, his life and work will in time become better known, and the memory of his name kept green by those who wage the unending struggle to make society more humane and just.

SIDNEY HOOK

New York University
August, 1963

THE present book has not only had its history, it has also in some way made a little history. Called forth by the circumstances described in the preface to the German edition, it created at its appearance a fair stir inside and outside German social democracy. Opponents of socialism declared it to be the most crushing testimony of the unsoundness of the socialist theory, and criticism of capitalist society and socialist writers. First of all Karl Kautsky denounced it as an abandonment of the fundamental principles and conception of scientific socialism. Induced by all this the German social democratic party put the book on the agenda of its Hanover Congress (October, 1899), where it was discussed in a debate that lasted three days and a half and ended with the acceptance of a resolution that was meant to be a rejection of the views put forward by the author.

I could not at that time take part in the debate. For political reasons I had to stay away from German territory. But I declared then that I regarded the excitement of my comrades over the book as the outcome of a state of nervous irritation created by the deductions the opponents of socialism drew from some of its sentences, and by an over-estimation of the importance to socialism of the tenets fought by me. But I could withdraw nothing, and although ten years have lapsed since, and I have now had seven years' most intimate knowledge of German political and economical conditions, I cannot yield on any material point. Subsequently the views put forward in the book have received the bye-name of REVISIONISM, and although some of those who are called REVISIONISTS in German social democracy hold on several points views different from mine, the book can, all in all, be regarded as an exposition of the theoretical and political tendencies of the German social democratic revisionists. It is widely read in Germany; only some weeks ago a new—the ninth—edition of it has been published.

For reasons explained in the preface to the first German edition the book is occasionally written in a rather hesitating way. But its principal aim will appear, I think, clear enough. It is the strong accentuation of what in Germany is called the GEGENWARTRARBEIT—the every-day work of the socialist party—that work in the furrows of the field which by many is regarded as mere stop-gap work compared with the great coming upheaval, and of which much has been done consequently in a half-hearted way only. Unable to believe in finalities at all, I cannot believe in a final aim of socialism. But I strongly believe in the socialist movement, in the march forward of the working classes, who step by step must work out their emancipation by changing society from the domain of a commercial land-holding oligarchy to a real democracy which in all its departments is guided by the interests of those who work and create.

ED. BERNSTEIN.

Berlin W. 30, *March 31st*, 1909.

PREFACE.

THE present work is substantially devoted to the establishment of ideas which the writer unfolded in a letter to the German Social Democratic Party assembled at Stuttgart from October 3rd to October 8th, 1898.

This letter reads :—

The views laid down by me in the series *Problems of Socialism* have lately been discussed in Socialist papers and meetings, and a request has been made that the Party of German Social Democrats should state its position in regard to them. In case this happens and the Party agrees to the request, I am induced to make the following explanation.

The vote of an assembly, however significant it may be, naturally cannot disconcert me in my views, which have been gained from an examination of social phenomena. What I wrote in the *Neue Zeit* is the expression of a conviction from which I do not find myself induced to depart in any important particular.

But it is just as natural that a vote of the party should find me anything but indifferent. And, therefore, it will be understood if I feel the paramount necessity of guarding myself against misconstruction of my conclusions and false deductions from them. As I am prevented from attending the Congress I send this written communication.

It has been maintained in a certain quarter that the practical deductions from my treatises would be the abandonment of the conquest of political power by the proletariat organised politically and economically. That is quite an arbitrary deduction, the accuracy of which I altogether deny.

I set myself against the notion that we have to expect shortly a collapse of the bourgeois economy, and that social democracy should be induced by the prospect of such an imminent, great, social catastrophe to adapt its tactics to that assumption. That I maintain most emphatically.

The adherents of this theory of a catastrophe, base it especially on the conclusions of the *Communist Manifesto*. This is a mistake in every respect.

The theory which the *Communist Manifesto* sets forth of the evolution of modern society was correct as far as it characterised the general tendencies of that evolution. But it was mistaken in several special deductions, above all in the estimate of the *time* the evolution would take. The last has been unreservedly acknowledged by Friedrich Engels, the joint author with Marx of the *Manifesto*, in his preface to the *Class War in France*. But it is evident that if social evolution takes a much greater period of time than was assumed, it must also take upon itself *forms* and lead to forms that were not foreseen and could not be foreseen then.

Social conditions have not developed to such an acute opposition of things and classes as is depicted in the *Manifesto*. It is not only useless, it is the greatest folly to attempt to conceal this from ourselves. The number of members of the possessing classes is to-day not smaller but larger. The enormous increase of social wealth is not accompanied by a decreasing number of large capitalists but by an increasing number of capitalists of all degrees. The middle classes change their character but they do not disappear from the social scale.

The concentration in productive industry is not being accomplished even to day in all its departments with equal thoroughness and at an equal rate. In a great many branches of production it certainly justifies the forecasts of the socialist critic of society; but in other branches it lags even to-day behind them. The process of concentration in agriculture proceeds still more slowly. Trade statistics show an extraordinarily elaborated graduation of enterprises in regard to size. No rung of the ladder is disappearing from it. The significant changes in the inner structure of these enterprises and their inter-relationship cannot do away with this fact.

In all advanced countries we see the privileges of the capitalist bourgeoisie yielding step by step to democratic organisations. Under the influence of this, and driven by the movement of the working classes which is daily becoming stronger, a social reaction has set in against the exploiting tendencies of capital, a counteraction which, although it still proceeds timidly and feebly, yet does exist, and is always drawing more departments of economic life under its influence. Factory legislation, the democratising of local government, and the extension of its area of work, the freeing of trade unions and systems of co-operative trading from legal restrictions, the consideration of standard conditions of labour in the work undertaken by public authorities—all these characterise this phase of the evolution.

But the more the political organisations of modern nations are democratised the more the needs and opportunities of great political catastrophes are diminished. He who holds firmly to the catastrophic theory of evolution must, with all his power, withstand and hinder the evolution described above, which, indeed, the logical defenders of that theory formerly did. But is the conquest of political power by the proletariat simply to be by a political catastrophe? Is it to be the appropriation and utilisation of the power of the State by the proletariat exclusively against the whole non-proletarian world?

He who replies in the affirmative must be reminded of two things. In 1872 Marx and Engels announced in the preface to the new edition of the *Communist Manifesto* that the Paris Commune had exhibited a proof that "the working classes cannot simply take possession of the ready-made State machine and set it in motion for their own aims." And in 1895 Friedrich Engels stated in detail in the preface to *War of the Classes* that the time of political surprises, of the "revolutions of small conscious minorities at the head of unconscious masses"

was to-day at an end, that a collision on a large
scale with the military would be the means of
checking the steady growth of social democracy
and of even throwing it back for a time—in
short, that social democracy would flourish far
better by lawful than by unlawful means and by
violent revolution. And he points out in conformity with this opinion that the next task of
the party should be " to work for an uninterrupted increase of its votes " or to carry on a
slow *propaganda of parliamentary activity*.

Thus Engels, who, nevertheless, as his
numerical examples show, still somewhat over-
estimated the rate of process of the evolution !
Shall we be told that he abandoned the conquest
of political power by the working classes, because he wished to avoid the steady growth of
social democracy secured by lawful means being
interrupted by a political revolution?

If not, and if one subscribes to his conclusions, one cannot reasonably take any offence
if it is declared that for a long time yet the task
of social democracy is, instead of speculating
on a great economic crash, " to organise the
working classes politically and develop them as
a democracy and to fight for all reforms in the
State which are adapted to raise the working
classes and transform the State in the direction
of democracy."

That is what I have said in my impugned
article and what I still maintain in its full
import. As far as concerns the question pro-
pounded above it is equivalent to Engel's
dictum, for democracy is, at any given time,

as much government by the working classes as
these are capable of practising according to
their intellectual ripeness and the degree of
social development they have attained. Engels,
indeed, refers at the place just mentioned to
the fact that the *Communist Manifesto* has
" proclaimed the conquest of the democracy
as one of the first and important tasks of the
fighting proletariat."

In short, Engels is so thoroughly convinced
that the tactics based on the presumption of a
catastrophe have had their day, that he even
considers a revision of them necessary in the
Latin countries where tradition is much more
favourable to them than in Germany. "If the
conditions of war between nations have altered,"
he writes, "no less have those for the war
between classes." Has this already been
forgotten?

No one has questioned the necessity for the
working classes to gain the control of government. The point at issue is between the theory
of a social cataclysm and the question whether
with the given social development in Germany
and the present advanced state of its working
classes in the towns and the country, a sudden
catastrophe would be desirable in the interest
of the social democracy. I have denied it and
deny it again, because in my judgment a greater
security for lasting success lies in a steady
advance than in the possibilities offered by a
catastrophic crash.

And as I am firmly convinced that important
periods in the development of nations cannot

be leapt over I lay the greatest value on the next tasks of social democracy, on the struggle for the political rights of the working man, on the political activity of working men in town and country for the interests of their class, as well as on the work of the industrial organisation of the workers.

In this sense I wrote the sentence that the movement means everything for me and that what is *usually* called "the final aim of socialism" is nothing; and in this sense I write it down again to-day. Even if the word "usually" had not shown that the proposition was only to be understood conditionally, it was obvious that it *could* not express indifference concerning the final carrying out of socialist principles, but only indifference—or, as it would be better expressed, carelessness—as to the form of the final arrangement of things. I have at no time had an excessive interest in the future, beyond general principles; I have not been able to read to the end any picture of the future. My thoughts and efforts are concerned with the duties of the present and the nearest future, and I only busy myself with the perspectives beyond so far as they give me a line of conduct for suitable action now.

The conquest of political power by the working classes, the expropriation of capitalists, are no ends in themselves but only means for the accomplishment of certain aims and endeavours. As such they are demands in the programme of social democracy and are not attacked by me. Nothing can be said beforehand as to the circumstances of their accomplishment; we can only fight for their realisation. But the conquest of political power necessitates the possession of political *rights*; and the most important problem of tactics which German social democracy has at the present time to solve, appears to me to be to devise the best ways for the extension of the political and economic rights of the German working classes.

The following work has been composed in the sense of these conclusions.

I am fully conscious that it differs in several important points from the ideas to be found in the theory of Karl Marx and Engels—men whose writings have exercised the greatest influence on my socialist line of thought, and one of whom—Engels—honoured me with his personal friendship not only till his death but who showed beyond the grave, in his testamentary arrangements, a proof of his confidence in me.

This deviation in the manner of looking at things certainly is not of recent date; it is the product of an inner struggle of years and I hold in my hand a proof that this was no secret to Friedrich Engels, and moreover I must guard Engels from the suspicion that he was so narrow-minded as to exact from his friends an unconditional adherence to his views. Nevertheless, it will be understood from the foregoing why I have till now avoided as much as possible giving to my deviating points of view the form of a systematic and detailed criticism of the Marx-Engels doctrine. This could the more easily be avoided up till now because as regards the practical questions with which we were concerned Marx and Engels in the course of time considerably modified their views.

All that is now altered. I have now a controversy with socialists who, like me, have sprung from the Marx-Engels school; and I am obliged, if I am to maintain my opinions, to show them the points where the Marx-Engels theory appears to me especially mistaken or to be self-contradictory.

I have not shirked this task, but, owing to the personal grounds already mentioned, it has not been easy to me. I acknowledge this openly so that the reader may not deduce uncertainty in the subject matter from the hesitating, clumsy form of the first chapters. I stand by what I have written with firm conviction; but I have not always succeeded in choosing the form and the arguments by means of which my thoughts would have gained the clearest expression. In this respect my work is far behind many a work published by others on the same subject. I have rectified in the last chapter some omissions in the first chapters. Further, as the publication of the work was somewhat delayed, the chapter on "Co-operation" has undergone some additions in which repetitions could not wholly be avoided.

For the rest, the work may speak for itself. I am not so ingenuous as to expect that it will forthwith convert those who have disagreed

with my previous essays, nor am I foolish
enough to wish that those who agree with me
in principle should subscribe to everything I
have said in it. In fact, the most doubtful side
of the work is that it embraces too much. When
I came to speak of the tasks of the present time
I was obliged, unless I wished to flounder into
generalities, to enter on all kinds of isolated
questions over which differences of opinion are
unavoidable even among those who otherwise
think alike. And yet the want of space compelled me to lay stress on some principal points
by implication rather than by establishing them.
But I repeat I am not concerned that others
should agree with me in every single question.
That which concerns me, that which forms the
chief aim of this work, is, by opposing what is
left of the utopian mode of thought in the
socialist theory, to strengthen equally the
realistic and the idealistic element in the socialist
movement.

ED. BERNSTEIN.

London, *January*, 1899.

Chapter I.

THE FUNDAMENTAL DOCTRINES OF MARXIST SOCIALISM.

(a) *The Scientific Elements of Marxism.*

" With them Socialism became a science which has now to be worked out in all its details and connections."—ENGELS : Herr Eugen Dühring's *Revolution in Science.*

German Social Democracy acknowledges to-day as the theoretical foundation of its activity the theory of society worked out by Marx and Engels and called by them scientific socialism. That is to say, that whilst Social Democracy, as a fighting party, supports certain interests and tendencies, it strives for aims set up by itself. In the designation of those aims it follows closely the methods of a science which is capable of an objective proof based only on an experience and logic to which it conforms. For what is not capable of such proof is no longer science but rests on subjective impulses, on mere desire or opinion.

In all sciences a distinction can be drawn between a pure and an applied science. The first consists of principles and of a knowledge, which are derived from the whole series of corresponding experiences and therefore looked upon as universally valid. They form the element of stability in the theory. From the application of these principles to single phenomena or to particular cases of practical experience, is formed an applied science; the knowledge won from this application put together in propositions forms the principles of the applied science. These form the variable element in the structure of a science.

The terms constant and variable are only to be taken here conditionally. For the principles of pure science are also subject to changes which, however, occur in the form of limitations. With advancing knowledge, propositions to which formerly absolute validity was attached are recognised as conditional and are supplemented by new scientific propositions which limit that validity, but which, at the same time, extend the domain of pure science. On the other hand single propositions of the applied science retain their validity for defined cases. A proposition in agricultural chemistry or electrical engineering in so far as it has been tested at all, always remains true as soon as the preliminary conditions on which it rests are restored. But the great number of the elements of these premises and their manifold possibilities of combination cause an infinite variety of such propositions and a constant shifting of their importance in relation to one another. Practice creates ever new materials of knowledge, and every day changes, so to say, its aspect as a whole, continually placing under the heading of outworn methods what was once a new acquisition.

A systematic stripping of its applied parts from the pure science of Marxist socialism has not hitherto been attempted, although important preparations for it are not wanting. Marx's well-known presentation of his conception of history in the preface of *A Contribution to the Criticism of Political Economy* and the third part of Fr. Engels' *Socialism, Utopian and Scientific* should be named here in the first place as being of the greatest importance. In the preface just mentioned Marx presents the general features of his philosophy of history and society in such concise and decisive sentences, so free from all reference to special phenomena and special forms, as has never been found elsewhere with equal clearness. No important thought concerning the Marxist philosophy of history is wanting there.

Engels' writing is partly a more popular drafting of Marx's propositions, partly an extension of them. Reference is made to special phenomena of social evolution, such as modern society, characterised by Marx as bourgeois society, and its further path of development is sketched out in more detail so that one, as regards many passages, can apply the term of applied science to it. Single details can be passed over without the fundamental thoughts suffering any damage. But in its principal propositions the presentation is still sufficiently general to be claimed for the pure science of Marxism. This is warranted and required by the fact that Marxism claims to be more than an abstract theory of history. It claims at the same time to be a theory of modern society and its development. If one wishes to discriminate very strictly, one could describe this part of the Marxist theory as an applied doctrine, but it is a thoroughly essential application of the Marxist theory without which it would lose nearly all significance as a political science. Therefore the general or chief propositions of these deductions regarding modern society must be ascribed to the pure doctrine of Marxism. If the present order of society resting legally on private property and free competition is a special case in the history of humanity, it is at the same time a general and lasting fact in the present civilised world. Everything in the Marxist characterisation of bourgeois society and its evolution which is unconditioned — that is, everything whose validity is free from national and local peculiarities—would accordingly belong to the domain of pure science; but everything that refers to temporary and local special phenomena and conjectures, all special forms of development, would on the other hand belong to applied science.

When we separate the fabric of the Marxist doctrine in the manner above named we are able to estimate the import of its separate propositions to the whole system. With every proposition of the pure science a portion of the foundation would be torn away and a great part of the whole building would be robbed of its support and fall down. But it is otherwise with the propositions of the applied science. These could fall without shaking the foundations in the least. A whole series of propositions in the applied science could fall without dragging down the other parts in sympathy.

Such a systematic division into the finer details lies, however, beyond the plan of this work, as it is not intended to be an exhaustive presentation and criticism of the Marxist philosophy. It suffices for my purpose to denote as the chief parts of what in my opinion is the building of the pure science of Marxism, the programme already mentioned of historical materialism, the theory (the germ of which is already contained therein) of the wars of the classes in general and the class war between bourgeoisie and proletariat in particular, as well as the theory of surplus value with that of the method of production in a bourgeois society and the description of the tendencies of the development of this society. Like the propositions of the applied science, those of the pure science are of different values to the system.

No one will deny that the most important element in the foundation of Marxism, the fundamental law so to say which penetrates the whole system, is its specific philosophy of history which bears the name of the materialist interpretation of history. With it Marxism stands or falls in principle; according to the measure in which it suffers limitations will the position of the other elements towards one another be affected in sympathy.

Every search into its validity must, therefore, start from the question whether or how far this theory is true.

(b) The Materialist Interpretation of History and Historic Necessity.

" We had to emphasise face to face with our opponents the chief principle (the economic side) denied by them, and there was not always time, place, and opportunity to do justice to the other considerations concerned in and affected by it."—FRIEDRICH ENGELS : Letter of 1890 reprinted in the *Sozialistischen Akademiker,* October, 1895.

The question of the correctness of the materialist interpretation of history is the question of the determining causes of historic necessity. To be a materialist means first of all to trace back all phenomena to the necessary movements of matter. These movements of matter are accomplished according to the materialist doctrine from beginning to end as a mechanical process, each individual process being the necessary result of preceding mechanical facts. Mechanical facts determine, in the last resort, all occurrences, even those which appear to be caused by ideas. It is, finally, always the movement of matter which determines the form of ideas and the directions of the will; and thus these also (and with them everything that happens in the world of humanity) are inevitable. The materialist is thus a Calvinist without God. If he does not believe in a predestination ordained by a divinity, yet he believes and must believe that starting from any chosen point of time all further events are, through the whole of existing matter and the directions of force in its parts, determined beforehand.

The application of materialism to the interpretation of history means then, first of all, belief in the inevitableness of all historical events and developments. The question is only, in what manner the inevitable is accomplished in human history, what element of force or what factors of force speak the decisive word, what is the relation of the different factors of force to one another, what part in history falls to the share of nature, of political economy, of legal organisations, of ideas.

Marx, in the already quoted passage, gives the answer, that he designates as the determining factor, the material productive forces and the conditions of production among men at the time. "The method of production of the material things of life settles generally the social, political, and spiritual process of life. It is not the consciousness of men that determines their mode of existence, but on the contrary their social existence that determines [the nature of] their consciousness. At a certain stage in their development the material productive forces of society come into opposition with the existing conditions of production or, which is only a legal expression for it, with the relations of property within which they have hitherto moved. From forms of development of the forces of production, these relations change into fetters. Then enters an epoch of social revolution. With the change of the economic foundation the whole gigantic super-structure (the legal and political organisations to which certain social forms of consciousness correspond) is more slowly or more quickly overthrown. One form of society never perishes before all the productive forces are evolved for which it is sufficiently comprehensive, and new or higher conditions of production never step on to the scene before the material conditions of existence of the same have come to light out of the womb of the old society. The bourgeois relations of production are the last antagonistic form of the social process of production . . . but the productive forces developing in the heart of the bourgeois society create at the same time the material conditions for the solution of this antagonism. The previous history of human society, therefore, terminates with this form of society.*

It must first be observed by anticipation that the concluding sentence and the word " last " in the preceding sentence are not capable of proof but are hypotheses more or less well founded. But they are not essential to the theory and even belong much more to the

---

* *A Contribution to the Criticism of Political Economy.* Preface.

applications of it, and they may therefore be passed over here.

If we look at the other sentences we are struck, above all, by their dogmatic wording, except the phrase the " more slowly or more quickly " (which indeed hides a good deal). In the second of the quoted sentences " consciousness " and " existence " are so sharply opposed that we are nearly driven to conclude that men were regarded solely as living agents of historical powers whose work they carry out positively against their knowledge and will. And this is only partly modified by a sentence omitted here as of secondary consideration in which is emphasised the need of discriminating in social revolutions between the material revolution in the conditions of production and the " ideologistic forms " in which men become conscious of this conflict and fight it out. On the whole the consciousness and will of men appear to be a very subordinate factor of the material movement.

In the preface to the first volume of *Capital* we come across a sentence savouring no less of predestination. " We are concerned," it reads, with reference to the " natural laws " of capitalist production, " with these tendencies working and forcing their way with iron necessity." And yet just when he was speaking of *law,* a milder concept comes forward—that of tendency. And on the next page stands the sentence so often quoted, that society can " shorten and soften " the birth pains of phases of development in conformity with nature.

The dependence of men on the conditions of production appears much more qualified in the explanation Friedrich Engels gives of historical materialism, during the lifetime of Karl Marx and in agreement with him, in his book against Dühring. There it reads that the " final causes of all social changes and political revolutions " are to be sought, not in the brains of men but " in changes of methods of production and exchange." But " final causes " includes concurrent causes of another kind—causes of the second or third degree, etc., and it is clear that the greater the series of such causes is, the more limited as to quantity and quality will be the determining power of the final causes. The fact of its action remains, but the final form of things does not depend on it alone. An issue which is the result of the working of different forces can only be reckoned upon with certainty when all the forces are exactly known and placed in the calculation according to their full value. The ignoring of a force of even a lower degree involves the greatest deviations, as every mathematician knows.

In his later works Engels has limited still further the determining force of the conditions of production—most of all in two letters reprinted in the *Sozialistischen Akademiker* of October, 1895, the one written in the year 1890, the other in the year 1894. There, " forms of law," political, legal, philosophical theories, religious intuitions or dogmas are enumerated as forces which influence the course of historical struggles and in many cases " are factors preponderating in the determination of their form." "There are then innumerable forces thwarting one another," we read, "an endless group of parallelograms of forces, from which one resultant—the historical event—is produced which itself can again be looked upon as the product of a power working as a whole without consciousness or will. For what every single man wills is hindered by every other man, and the result of the struggle is something which no one had intended." (Letter of 1890.) "The political, legal, philosophical, religious, literary, artistic evolution rests on the economic evolution. But they all react on one another and on the economic basis." (Letter of 1895.) It must be confessed that this sounds somewhat differently from the passage from Marx quoted above.

It will, of course, not be maintained that Marx and Engels at any time overlooked the fact that non-economic factors exercise an influence on the course of history. Innumerable passages from their early writings can be quoted against such suppositions. But we are dealing here with a question of proportion—not whether ideologic factors were acknowledged, but what measure of influence, what significance for history were ascribed to them, and in this respect it cannot be denied that Marx and Engels originally assigned to the non-economic factors a much less influence on the evolution of society, a much less power of modifying by their action the conditions of production than in their later writings. This corresponds also to the natural course of the development of every new theory. Such an one always first appears in sharp categoric formulation. In order to gain authority, the untenability of the old theory must be shown, and in this conflict one-sidedness and exaggeration are easily manifested. In the sentence which we placed as a motto to this section of the volume, Engels acknowledges it unreservedly, and in the following sentence he remarks : '' It is unfortunately only too common for a man to think he has perfectly understood a theory and is able forthwith to apply it, as soon as he has made the chief propositions his own.'' He who to-day employs the materialist theory of history is bound to employ it in its most developed, not in its original, form—that is, he is bound in addition to the development and influence of the productive forces and conditions of production to make full allowance for the ideas of law and morals, the historical and religious traditions of every epoch, the influences of geographical and other circumstances of nature—to which also the nature of man himself and his spiritual disposition belong. This must be kept quite particularly in view when it is a question no longer of simple research into earlier epochs of history, but of foretelling coming developments, if the materialist conception of history is to be of use as a guide to the future.

In a letter to Conrad Schmidt dated October 27th, 1890, Friedrich Engels showed in an excellent manner how from being products of economic development, social institutions

become independent social forces with actions of
their own, which in their turn may react on the
former, and according to circumstances,
promote or hinder them or turn them into other
directions. He brings forward in the first place
the power of the state as an example, when he
completes the definition of the state mostly given
by him—as the organ of the *government of the
classes* and of *repression*—by the very important
derivation of the state from the social division
of labour.* Historical materialism by no means
denies every autonomy to political and ideologic
forces—it combats only the idea that these
independent actions are unconditional, and
shows that the development of the economic
foundations of social life—the conditions of
production and the evolution of classes—finally
exercises the stronger influence on these actions.

But in any case the multiplicity of the factors
remains, and it is by no means always easy to
lay bare the relations which exist among them
so exactly that it can be determined with certainty where in given cases the strongest
motive power is to be sought. The purely
economic causes create, first of all, only a disposition for the reception of certain ideas, but
how these then arise and spread and what form
they take, depend on the co-operation of a
whole series of influences. More harm than

---

* Certainly in the *Origin of the Family* it is shown in
detail how the social division of labour makes the rise of
the state necessary. But Engels lets this side of the
origin of the state fall completely, and finally treats the
state, as in *Anti-Dühring*, as only the organ of political
repression.

good is done to historical materialism if at the outset one rejects as eclecticism an accentuation of the influences other than those of a purely economic kind, and a consideration of other economic factors than the technics of production and their foreseen development. Eclecticism—the selecting from different explanations and ways of dealing with phenomena—is often only the natural reaction from the doctrinaire desire to deduce everything from one thing and to treat everything according to one and the same method. As soon as such desire is excessive the eclectic spirit works its way again with the power of a natural force. It is the rebellion of sober reason against the tendency inherent in every doctrine to fetter thought.

Now, to whatever degree other forces besides the purely economic, influence the life of society, just so much more also does the sway of what, in an objective sense, we call historic necessity change. In modern society we have to distinguish in this respect two great streams. On the one side appears an increasing insight into the laws of evolution and notably of economic evolution. With this knowledge goes hand in hand, partly as its cause, partly again as its effect, an increasing capability of *directing* the economic evolution. The economic natural force, like the physical, changes from the ruler of mankind to its servant according as its nature is recognised. Society, theoretically, can be freer than ever in regard to the economic movement, and only the antagonism of interests among its elements—the power of private and

group elements—hinders the full transition of
freedom from theory to practice. Yet the common interest gains in power to an increasing
extent as opposed to private interest, and the
elementary sway of economic forces ceases
according to the degree in which this is the case,
and in all places where this is the case. Their
development is anticipated and is therefore
accomplished all the more quickly and easily.
Individuals and whole nations thus withdraw
an ever greater part of their lives from the
influence of a necessity compelling them, without
or against their will.

But because men pay ever greater attention
to economic factors it easily appears as though
these played a greater part to-day than formerly. That, however, is not the case. The
deception is only caused because in many cases
the economic motive appears freely to-day
where formerly it was concealed by conditions of
government and symbols of all kinds. Modern
society is much richer than earlier societies in
ideologics which are not determined by economics and by nature working as an economic
force. Sciences, arts, a whole series of social
relations are to-day much less dependent on
economics than formerly, or, in order to give
no room for misconception, the point of
economic development attained to-day leaves the
ideological, and especially the ethical, factors
greater space for independent activity than was
formerly the case. In consequence of this the
interdependency of cause and effect between
technical, economic evolution, and the evolution

of other social tendencies is becoming always more indirect, and from that the necessities of the first are losing much of their power of dictating the form of the latter.

" The Iron Necessity of History " receives in this way a limitation, which, let me say at once, signifies in regard to the practice of social democracy, no lessening but an increasing and qualifying of its social political tasks.

Thus we see the materialist conception of history to-day in another form than it was presented at first by its founders. It has gone through a development already, it has suffered limitations in absolutist interpretation. That is, as has been shown, the history of every theory. It would be the greatest retrogression to go back from the ripe form which Engels has given it in the letters to Conrad Schmidt to the first definitions and to give it a " monistic " interpretation based on these.

The first definitions are rather to be supplemented by those letters. The fundamental idea of the theory does not thereby lose in uniformity, but the theory itself gains in scientific character. Only with these supplements does it become truly a theory of the scientific treatment of history. In its first form it could become in the hand of a Marx a lever of mighty historical discoveries, but even his genius was led by it to all kinds of false conclusions.*

---

* " It is much easier," says Marx in a much-quoted passage in *Capital*, " to find by analyses the earthly kernel of religious, hazy imaginations than by the reverse process to evolve from the actual conditions of life their

Finally, the question arises, up to what point the materialist conception of history has a claim to its name, if we continue to widen it in the above-mentioned manner through the inclusion of other forces. In fact, according to Engels' explanations, it is not purely materialist, much less purely economic. I do not deny that the name does not completely fit the thing. But I seek progress not in making ideas confused, but in making them precise; and because it is of primary importance in the characterisation of a theory of history to acknowledge in what it differs from others, I would, far from taking offence at the title "Economic Interpretation of History," keep it, in spite of all that can be said against it, as the most appropriate description of the Marxist theory of history.

Its significance rests on the weight it lays on economics; out of the recognition and valuation of economic facts arise its just services to the science of history, and the enrichment which this branch of human knowledge owes to it. An economic interpretation of history does not necessarily mean that only economic forces, only economic motives, are recognised; but only that economics forms an ever recurring decisive force, the cardinal point of the great movements in history. To the words "materialist conception

---

heavenly form. The latter is the only materialistic and therefore scientific method " (*Capital*, I., 2nd ed., p. 386). In this contrast there is great exaggeration. Unless one already knew the heavenly forms, the method of deduction described would lead to all kinds of arbitrary constructions, and if one knew them the deduction described is a means of scientific analysis, but not a scientific antithesis to analytic interpretation.

of history" still adhere all the misunderstandings which are closely joined with the conception of materialism. Philosophic materialism, or the materialism of natural science, is in a mechanical sense deterministic. The Marxist conception of history is not. It allots to the economic foundation of the life of nations no unconditioned determining influence on the forms this life takes.

(c) The Marxist Doctrine of Class War and of the Evolution of Capital.

The doctrine of the class wars rests on the foundation of the materialist conception of history. " It was found," writes Engels in *Anti-Dühring*, " that all history* hitherto was the history of class wars, that the classes fighting each other are, each time, the outcome of the conditions of production and commerce— in one word, of the economic conditions of their epoch " (3rd edition, page 12). In modern society it is the class war between the capitalist owners of the means of production and the producers without capital, the wage workers, which imprints its mark on history in this respect. For the former class Marx took from France the term BOURGEOISIE, and for the latter the term PROLETARIAT. This class struggle between bourgeoisie and proletariat is accordingly the antagonism, transferred to men, which is in the conditions of production to-day, that

---

* In the fourth edition of the work *Socialism, Utopian and Scientific*, follow here the limiting words "with the exception of primitive societies."

is, in the private character of the method of
appropriation and the social character of the
method of production. The means of production
are the property of individual capitalists who
appropriate to themselves the results of the
production, but the production itself has become
a social process; that means, a production of
commodities for use made by many workers on
a basis of systematic division and organisation
of labour. And this antagonism conceals in
itself, or has, a second conflict, as a supplement:
the systematic division and organisation of
work within the establishments for production
(workshop, factory, combination of factories,
etc.) is opposed by the unsystematic disposal of
the produce on the market.

The starting point of the class struggle
between capitalists and workers is the antagonism of interests which follows from the nature
of the utilisation of the labour of the latter by
the former for profit. The examination of this
process of utilisation leads to the doctrine of
value and of the production and appropriation
of *surplus value.*

It is significant for capitalist production and
the order of society founded thereon, that men
in their economic relations stand opposed to one
another throughout as buyers and sellers. It
recognises in social life no general legal relations of dependence but only actual ones following from purely economic relations (differences
of economic means, relation of hirer and hired,
etc.). The worker sells to the capitalist his
power to work for a definite time, under definite

conditions, and for a definite price—wages. The capitalist sells the products (manufactured with the help of the worker—that is, by the whole of the workers employed by him) in the goods market at a price which, as a rule and as a condition of the continuance of his undertaking, yields a surplus above the amount which the manufacture costs. What is, then, this surplus?

According to Marx it is the surplus value of the labour accomplished by the worker. The goods are exchanged on the market at a value which is fixed by the labour embodied in them, measured according to time. What the capitalist has put in in past—we would even say dead—labour in the form of raw material, auxiliary material, wear and tear of machinery, rent, and other costs of production, appears again unchanged in the value of the product. It is otherwise with the living work expended on it. This costs the capitalist wages; it brings him an amount beyond these, the equivalent of the value of labour. The labour value is the value of the quantity of labour worked into the product; the worker's wages is the selling price of the labour power used up in production. Prices, or the value of labour power, are determined by the cost of maintenance of the worker as it corresponds with his historically developed habits of life. The difference between the equivalent (*erlös*) of the labour-value and the labour-wage is the surplus value which it is the natural endeavour of the capitalist to raise as high as possible and in any case not to allow to sink.

But competition on the market of commodities presses constantly on the price of commodities, and an increase of sales is again only obtained by a cheapening of production. The capitalist can attain this cheapening in three kinds of ways : lowering of wages, lengthening of the hours of work, an increase in the productivity of labour. As at a given time there are always definite limits to the first two, his energy is always being turned to the last one. Better organisation of work, inter-unification of work and perfecting of machinery are, in the more developed capitalist societies, the predominating means of cheapening production. In all these cases the consequence is that the organic *composition of capital*, as Marx calls it, is changing. The relation of the portion of capital laid out in raw materials, tools for work, etc., increases ; the portion of capital laid out in labour wages decreases ; the same amount of commodities is produced by fewer workers, an increased amount by the old or even by a less number of workers. The ratio of the surplus value to the portion of capital laid out in wages Marx calls the rate of surplus value or of exploitation, the ratio of the surplus value to the whole capital invested in producing he calls the rate of profit. From the foregoing it is self-evident that the rate of surplus can rise at the same time as the rate of profit falls.

According to the nature of the branch of production we find a very different organic combination of capital. There are undertakings where a disproportionately large portion of the capital is spent on instruments of work, raw material, etc., and only a relatively small amount on wages; and others where the wages form the most important part of the expenditure of capital. The first represent higher, the second lower, organic combinations of capital. If an equal proportionate rate ruled throughout between the surplus value attained and the labour wage, in these latter branches of production the profit rates would in many cases exceed those in the first by multiples. But that is not the case. In a developed capitalist society goods are sold not at their labour values but at their prices of production, which consist of the cost of production (workers' wages plus dead work used up) and of an additional expense which corresponds with the average profit of the whole social production, or the profit rate of that branch of production in which the organic combination of capital shows an average ratio of wages-capital to capital employed for the other purposes. The prices of commodities in the different branches of production, therefore, show by no means the same relation to their value. In some cases they are constantly far below the value, and in others constantly above it, and only in those branches of production with an average composition of capital do they approach the value. The law of value disappears altogether from the consciousness of the producers; it works only behind their backs, whilst the level of the average profit rate is regulated by it at longer intervals only.

The coercive laws of competition and the

growing wealth of capital in society tend to lower constantly the profit rate, whilst this is delayed by forces working in opposite directions but is not permanently stopped. Overproduction of capital goes hand in hand with forces creating a superabundance of workers. Greater centralisation is always spreading in manufactures, commerce, and agriculture, and an expropriation of the smaller capitalists by the greater grows. Periodic crises brought about by the anarchy in production in conjunction with the under-consumption of the masses are always reappearing in a more violent and more destructive character; and they hasten the process of centralisation and expropriation by the ruin of innumerable small capitalists. On the one side is generalised the collective—co-operative—form of the process of work on an always growing scale, in an ascending degree; on the other side increases "with the constantly diminishing number of capitalist magnates who usurp and monopolise all the advantages of this process of transformation, the mass of misery, oppression, servitude, deterioration, exploitation, but also with it the revolt of the working class constantly increasing and taught, united and organised by the mechanism of the capitalist process of production itself." Thus the development reaches a point where the monopoly of capital becomes a fetter to the method of production that has thriven on it, when the centralisation of the means of production and the socialisation of labour become incompatible with their capitalist garment.

This is then rent. The expropriators and usurpers are expropriated by the mass of the nation. Capitalist private property is done away with.

This is the historical tendency of the manner of production and appropriation, according to Marx. The class which is called upon to carry out the expropriation of the capitalist class and the transformation of capitalist into public property, is the class of the wage earners, the proletariat. For this purpose must the class be organised as a political party. This party at a given moment seizes the power of the State and "changes the means of production first of all into State property. But therewith the proletariat negatives itself as a proletariat, therewith it puts an end to all differences of class and antagonisms of class, and consequently also puts an end to the State as a State." The struggle for individual existence with its conflicts and excesses is over, the State has nothing more to oppress "and dies off."*

*   *   *

So far, in the most concise compression possible, I have endeavoured to set forth the most important propositions of that part of the Marxist theory which we have to consider as essential to his socialism. Just as little as—or, rather, still less than—the materialist theory of history has this part of the theory sprung from the beginning in a perfected form from the head of its authors. Even more than in the former

---

* Engels, *Socialism, Utopian and Scientific.*

case can a development of the theory be shown which, whilst firmly maintaining the chief points of view, consists of limiting the propositions at first represented as absolute. In the preface to *Capital* (1867), in the preface to the new edition of the *Communist Manifesto* (1872), in the preface and a note to the new edition of the *Poverty of Philosophy* (1884), and in the preface to the *Class Struggles in the French Revolution* (1895), some of the changes are shown which in the course of time have been brought to pass with regard to various corresponding matters in the views of Marx and Engels. But not all the changes to be cited here and elsewhere with reference to single portions or hypotheses of the theory have found full consideration in its final elaboration. Marx and Engels confined themselves sometimes merely to hinting at, sometimes only to stating in regard to single points, the changes recognised by them in facts, and in the better analyses of these facts, which influenced the form and application of their theory. And even in the last respect contradictions are not wanting in their writings. They have left to their successors the duty of bringing unity again into their theory and of co-ordinating theory and practice.

But this duty can only be accomplished if one gives an account unreservedly of the gaps and contradictions in the theory. In other words, the *further development and elaboration of the Marxist doctrine must begin with criticism of it.* To-day, the position is that one can prove *everything* out of Marx and Engels. This is very comfortable for the apologists and the literary pettifogger. But he who has kept only a moderate sense for theory, for whom the scientific character of socialism is not " only a show-piece which on festive occasions is taken out of a plate cupboard but otherwise is not taken into consideration," he, as soon as he is conscious of these contradictions, feels also the need of removing them. The duty of the disciples consists in doing this and not in everlastingly repeating the words of their masters.

In this sense has been undertaken the following criticism of some elements of the Marxist doctrine. The wish to keep within moderate bounds a volume intended in the first instance for the use of working men, and the necessity of finishing it within a few weeks explain why an exhaustive treatment of the subject has not even been attempted. At the same time, let it be understood once for all that no pretensions are raised as to originality in the criticism. Most, if not all, of what follows has in substance been worked out—or at least indicated—by others already. The justification for this essay is not that it discloses something not known before but that it acknowledges what has been disclosed already.

But this is also a necessary work. The mistakes of a theory can only be considered as overcome when they are recognised as such by the advocates of that theory. Such recognition does not necessarily signify the destruction of

the theory. It may rather appear after sub-
traction of what is acknowledged to be mistaken
—if I may be allowed to use an image of
Lassalle—that it is Marx finally who carries
the point against Marx.

CHAPTER II.

THE ECONOMIC DEVELOPMENT OF MODERN SOCIETY.

(a) *On the Meaning of the Marxist Theory of Value.*

" From which incidentally the practical application follows that there are sometimes difficulties with the popular claim of the worker to the " full proceeds of his labour."
—ENGELS, *Herr Eugen Dühring's Unwälzung.*

According to the Marxist theory surplus value is, as we have seen, the pivot of the economy of a capitalist society. But in order to understand surplus value one must first know what value is. The Marxist representation of history and of the course of development of capitalist society begins therefore with the analysis of value.

In modern society, according to Marx, the value of commodities consists in the socially necessary labour spent on them measured according to time. But with the analysis of this measure of value quite a series of abstractions and reductions is necessary. First, the pure exchange value must be found; that is, we must leave aside the special use values of the particular commodities. Then—in forming the concept of general or abstract human labour—we must allow for the peculiarities of particular kinds of labour (reducing higher or complex labour to simple or abstract labour). Then, in order to attain to the socially necessary time of work as a measure of the value of labour, we must allow for the differences in diligence, activity, equipment of the individual workers; and, further (as soon as we are concerned with the transformation of value into market value, or price), for the socially necessary labour time required for the particular commodities separately. But the value of labour thus gained demands a new reduction. In a capitalistic developed society commodities, as has already been mentioned, are sold not according to their individual value but according to their price of production—that is, the actual cost price plus an average proportional rate of profit whose degree is determined by the ratio of the total value of the whole social production to the total wage of human labour power expended in producing, exchanging, etc. At the same time the ground rent must be deducted from the total value, and the division of the capital into industrial, commercial, and bank capital must be taken into the calculation.

In this way, as far as single commodities or a category of commodities comes into consideration, value loses every concrete quality and becomes a pure abstract concept. But what becomes of the surplus value under these circumstances? This consists, according to the Marxist theory, of the difference between the labour value of the products and the payment for the labour force spent in their production by the workers. It is therefore evident that at the moment when labour value can claim acceptance only as a speculative formula or scientific hypothesis, surplus value would all the more become a pure formula—a formula which rests on an hypothesis.

As is known, Friedrich Engels in an essay left behind him which was published in the *Neue Zeit* of the year 1895-96, pointed out a solution of the problem through the historical consideration of the process. Accordingly the law of value was of a directly determining power, it directly governed the exchange of commodities in the period of exchange and barter of commodities preceding the capitalist order of society.

Engels seeks to prove this in connection with a passage in the third volume of *Capital* by a short description of the historic evolution of economics. But although he presents the rise and development of the rate of profit so brilliantly, the essay fails in convincing strength of proof just where it deals with the question of value. According to Engels' representation the Marxist law of value ruled generally as an economic law from five to seven thousand years, from the beginning of exchanging products as commodities (in Babylon, Egypt, etc.) up to the beginning of the era of capitalist production. Parvus, in a number of *Neue Zeit* of the same year, made good some conclusive objections to this view by pointing to a series of facts (feudal relations, undifferentiated agriculture, monopolies of guilds, etc.) which hindered the conception of a general exchange value founded on the labour time of the producers. It is quite clear that exchange on the basis of labour value cannot be a general rule so long as production for exchange is only an auxiliary branch of the industrial units, viz., the utilisation of surplus labour, etc., and as long as the conditions under which the exchanging producers take part in the act of exchange are fundamentally different. The problem of Labour forming exchange value and the connected problems of value and surplus value is no clearer at that stage of industry than it is to-day.

But what was at those times clearer than to-day is the fact of surplus labour. When surplus labour was performed in ancient time— and in the middle ages no kind of deception prevailed about it—it was not hidden by any conception of value. When the slave had to produce for exchange he was a simple surplus labour machine. The serf and the bondsman performed surplus labour in the open form of compulsory service (duties in kind, tithes, etc.). The journeyman employed by the guildmaster could easily see what his work cost his master, and at how much he reckoned it to his customer.*

---

* Where pre-capitalist methods of industry have been handed down to present times, surplus labour is shown to-day even unconcealed. The man employed by the small builder who performs a piece of work for one of his customers knows quite well that his hour's wage is so much less than the price which the master puts in his account for the hour's work. The same with the customers of tailors, gardeners, etc.

This clearness of the relations between wages of labour and price of commodities prevails even on the threshold of the capitalist period. From it are explained many passages that surprise us to-day in the economic writings of that time about surplus labour and labour as the sole producer of weath. What appears to us the result of a deeper observation of things was at the time almost a commonplace. It did not at all occur to the rich of that epoch to represent their riches as the fruit of their own work. The theory arising at the beginning of the manufacturing period of labour as the measure of exchange value (the latter conception then first becoming general) certainly starts from the conception of labour as the only parent of wealth, and interprets value still quite concretely (viz., as the cost price of a commodity), but forthwith contributes more towards confusing the conceptions of surplus labour than of clearing them. We can learn from Marx himself how Adam Smith, on the basis of these conceptions, represented profits and ground rent as deductions from the labour value; how Ricardo worked out this thought more fully, and how socialists turned it against the bourgeois economy.

But with Adam Smith labour value is already conceived as an abstraction from the prevailing reality. His full reality is in "the early and crude state of society" which precedes the accumulation of capital and the appropriation of land, and in backward industries. In the capitalist world, on the other hand, profit and

rent are for Smith constituent elements of
value beside labour or wages ; and labour value
serves Smith only as a " concept " to disclose
the division of the products of labour—that is
the fact of surplus labour.

In the Marxist system it is not otherwise in
principle. Marx certainly sticks to the idea of
labour value more firmly than Smith, and has
conceived it in a more strict but at the same
time also more abstract form. But whilst the
Marxist school — and the present author
amongst them—believed that a point of fundamental importance for the system was the
passionately discussed question as to whether
the attribute of " socially necessary labour
time " in labour value related only to the
manner of the production of the respective
commodities or included also the relation of
the *amount* produced of these commodities
to effective demand, a solution lay already
in the desk of Marx which gave quite a different complexion to this and other questions,
forced it into another region, on to another
plane. The value of individual commodities or
kinds of commodities becomes something quite
secondary, since they are sold at the price of
their production—cost of production plus profit
rate. What takes the first place is the *value
of the total production of society*, and the excess
of this value over the total amount of the wages
of the working classes—that is, not the individual, but the total social surplus value. That
which the whole of the workers produce in a
given moment over the portion falling to their

share, forms the social surplus value, the surplus value of the social production which the individual capitalists share in approximately equal proportion according to the amount of capital applied by them for business purposes. But the amount of this surplus value is only realised in proportion to the relation between the total production and the total demand—*i.e.*, the buying capacity of the market. From this point of view—that is, taking *production as a whole*—the value of every single kind of commodity is determined by the labour time which was necessary to produce it under normal conditions of production to that amount which the market—that is the community as purchasers—can take in each case. Now just for the commodities under consideration there is in reality no exact measure of the need of the community at a given moment; and thus value conceived as above is a purely abstract entity, not otherwise than the value of the final utility of the school of Gossen, Jevons, and Böhm-Bawerk. Actual relations lie at the foundation of both; but both are built up on abstractions.

Such abstractions naturally cannot be avoided in the observation of complex phenomena. How far they are admissible depends entirely on the substance and the purpose of the investigation. At the outset, Marx takes so much away from the characteristics of commodities that they finally remain only embodiments of a quantity of simple human labour; as to the Böhm-Jevons school, it takes away all characteristics except utility. But the one and the other kind of abstractions are only admissible for definite purposes of demonstration, and the propositions found by virtue of them have only worth and validity within defined limits.

If there exist no exact measure for the total demand at one time of a certain class of commodities, practical experience shows that within certain intervals of time the demand and supply of all commodities approximately equalise themselves. Practice shows, further, that in the production and distribution of commodities only a part of the community takes an active share, whilst another part consists of persons who either enjoy an income for services which have no direct relation to the production or have an income without working at all. An essentially greater number of men thus live on the labour of all those employed in production than are engaged actively in it, and income statistics show us that the classes not actively engaged in production appropriate, moreover, a much greater share of the total produced than the relation of their number to that of the actively producing class. The surplus labour of the latter is an empiric fact, demonstrable by experience, which needs no deductive proof. Whether the Marxist theory of value is correct or not is quite immaterial to the proof of surplus labour. It is in this respect no demonstration but only a means of analysis and illustration.

If, then, Marx presumes, in the analysis of the production of commodities, that single commodities are sold at their value, he illustrates on a single object the transaction which, according to his conception, the total production actually presents. The labour time spent on the whole of the commodities is in the sense before indicated, their social value.*

And even if this social value is not fully realised—because a depreciation of commodities is always occurring through partial over-production—yet this has in principle no bearing on the fact of the social surplus value or surplus product. The growth of its amount will be occasionally hindered or made slower, but there is no question of it standing still, much less of a retrogression in its amount in any modern state.

The surplus product is everywhere increasing, but the ratio of its increase to the increase of wages-capital is declining to-day in the more advanced countries.

By the simple fact that Marx applies the formula for the value of the whole of the commodities, to single commodities, it is already indicated that he makes the formation of surplus value fall exclusively in the sphere of production, where it is the industrial wage earner who produces it. All other active

* It is, in fact, the law of value . . . that not only on every single commodity is just the necessary labour time spent, but that no more than the necessary proportional amount of the social total labour time is spent in the different groups. " For use value is the condition . . . the social need—that is, the use value on a social basis appears here as the determining factor for the shares of the total social labour time which fall to the lot of the different particular spheres of production " (*Capital*, III., 2, pp. 176, 177). This sentence alone makes it impossible to make light of the Gossen-Böhm theory with a few superior phrases.

elements in modern economic life are auxiliary
agents to production and indirectly help to
raise the surplus value when they, for example,
as merchants, bankers, etc., or their staff,
undertake services for industry which would
otherwise fall upon it, and so they lessen its
cost. The wholesale dealers, etc., with their
employees, are only transformed and differentiated clerks, etc., of the industrial *entrepreneurs,* and their profits are the transformed
and concentrated charges of the latter. The
employees for wages of these merchants certainly create surplus value for them, but no
social surplus value. For the profit of their
employers, together with their own wages,
form a portion of the surplus value which is
produced in the industry. Only, this share is
then proportionately less than it was before the
differentiation of the functions here under consideration or than it would be without it. This
differentiation only renders possible the great
development of production on a large scale and
the acceleration of the turnover of industrial
capital. Like division of labour generally, it
raises the productivity of industrial capital,
relatively to the labour directly employed in
industry.

We limit ourselves to this short recapitu-
lation of the exposition of mercantile capital
(from which, again, banking capital represents
a differentiation) and of mercantile profit set
forth in the third volume of *Capital.*

It is clear from this within what narrow
limits the labour that creates supply value is

conceived in the Marxist system. The functions developed, as also others not discussed here, are from their nature indispensable to the social life of modern times. Their forms can, and undoubtedly will, be altered; but they themselves will in substance remain, as long as mankind does not dissolve into small social self-contained communities, when they then might be partly annulled and partly reduced to a minimum. In the theory of value which holds good for the society of to-day the whole expenditure for these functions is represented plainly as a deduction from surplus value, partly as "charges," partly as a component part of the rate of exploitation.

There is here a certain arbitrary dealing in the valuing of functions in which the actual community is no longer under consideration, but a supposititious, socially-managed community. This is the key to all obscurities in the theory of value. It is only to be understood with the help of this model. We have seen that surplus value can only be grasped as a concrete fact by thinking of the whole economy of society. Marx did not succeed in finishing the chapter on the classes that is so important for his theory. In it would have been shown most clearly that labour value is nothing more than a key, an abstract image, like the philosophical atom endowed with a soul—a key which, employed by the master hand of Marx, has led to the exposure and presentation of the mechanism of capitalist economy as this had not been hitherto treated, not so forcibly, logically, and clearly. But this key refuses service over and above a certain point, and therefore it has become disastrous to nearly every disciple of Marx.

The theory of labour value is above all misleading in this that it always appears again and again as the measure of the actual exploitation of the worker by the capitalist, and among other things, the characterisation of the rate of surplus value as the rate of exploitation reduces us to this conclusion. It is evident from the foregoing that it is false as such a measure, even when one starts from society as a whole and places the total amount of workers' wages against the total amount of other incomes. The theory of value gives a norm for the justice or injustice of the partition of the product of labour just as little as does the atomic theory for the beauty or ugliness of a piece of sculpture. We meet, indeed, to-day the best placed workers, members of the " aristocracy of labour," just in those trades with a very high rate of surplus value, the most infamously ground-down workers in others with a very low rate.

A scientific basis for socialism or communism cannot be supported on the fact only that the wage worker does not receive the full value of the product of his work. " Marx," says Engels, in the preface to the *Poverty of Philosophy,* " has never based his communistic demands on this, but on the necessary collapse of the capitalist mode of production which is being daily more nearly brought to pass before our eyes."

Let us see how in this respect the matter stands.

(b) The Distribution of Wealth in the Modern Community.

" If on the one side accumulation appears as growing concentration . . . on the other side it appears as the repulsion of individual capitalists from one another."—MARX, *Capital*, I., 4th ed., p. 590.

The capitalist, according to the theory of Marx, must produce surplus value in order to obtain a profit, but he can only draw surplus value from living labour. In order to secure the market against his competitors he must strive after a cheapening of production and this he attains, where the lowering of wages is resisted, only by means of an increase of the productivity of labour; that is by the perfecting of machinery and the economising of human labour. But in reducing human labour he places so much labour producing surplus value out of its function, and so kills the goose that lays the golden egg. The consequence is a gradually accomplished lowering of the profit rate, which through counteracting circumstances, is certainly temporarily hindered, but is always starting again. This produces another intrinsic contradiction in the capitalist mode of production. Profit rate is the inducement to the productive application of capital; if it falls below a certain point, the motive for productive undertakings is weakened—especially as far as concerns the new amounts of capital which enter the market as off-shoots of the accumulated masses of capital. Capital shows itself as a barrier to capitalist production. The continued development of production is interrupted. Whilst on the one hand every active particle of capital tries to secure and increase its rate of profit by means of a feverish strain of production, congestion in the expansion of production already sets in on the other. This is only the counterpart of the transactions leading to relative over-production, which produces a crisis in the market of use values. Over-production of commodities is at the same time manifesting itself as over-production of capital. Here as there, crises bring about a temporary arrangement. Enormous depreciation and destruction of capital take place, and under the influence of stagnation a portion of the working class must submit to a reduction of wages below the average, as an increased reserve army of superabundant hands stands at the disposal of capital in the labour market.

Thus after a time the conditions of a profitable investment of capital are re-established and the dance can go on anew but with the intrinsic contradiction already mentioned on an increased scale. Greater centralisation of capital, greater concentration of enterprises, increased rate of exploitation.

Now, is all that right?

Yes and no. It is true above all as a tendency. The forces painted are there and work in the given direction. And the proceedings are also taken from reality. The fall of the profit rate is a fact, the advent of over-production and crises is a fact, periodic diminution of capital is a fact, the concentration and centralisation of industrial capital is a fact, the increase of the rate of surplus value is a fact. So far we are, in principle, agreed in the statement. When the statement does not agree with reality it is not because something false is said, but because what is said is incomplete. Factors which influence the contradictions described by limiting them, are in Marx either quite ignored, or are, although discussed at some place, abandoned later on when the established facts are summed up and confronted, so that the social result of the conflicts appears much stronger and more abrupt than it is in reality.

Unfortunately there is a lack everywhere of exhaustive statistics to show the actual division of the shares, the preference shares, etc., of the limited companies which to-day form so large a portion of the social capital, as in most countries they are anonymous (that is like other paper money, they can change owners without formalities); whilst in England, where the shares registered in names predominate and the list of shareholders thus determined can be inspected by anyone in the State Registry Office, the compilation of more exact statistics of the owners of shares is a gigantic labour on which no one has yet ventured. One can only approximately estimate their number by reference to certain information collected about individual companies. Still, in order to show how very deceptive are the ideas which are formed in this direction and how the most modern and crass form of capitalist centralisation—the "Trust"—has in fact quite a different effect on the distribution of wealth from what it seems to outsiders to possess, the following figures which can be easily verified are given :—

The English Sewing Thread Trust, formed about a year ago,* counts no less than 12,300 shareholders. Of these there are 6,000 holders of original shares with £60 average capital, 4,500 holders of preference shares with £150 average capital, 1,800 holders of debentures with £315 average capital. Also the Trust of the spinners of fine cotton had a respectable number of shareholders, namely 5,454. Of these, there were 2,904 holders of original shares with £300 average capital, 1,870 holders of preference shares with £500 average capital, 680 holders of debentures with £130 average capital.

With the Cotton Trust of J. and P. Coates it is similar. †

The shareholders in the great Manchester Canal amount in round numbers to 40,000, those in the large provision company of T. Lipton to 74,262. A stores business in London, Spiers and Pond, instanced as a recent example

---

* Written 1899.

† In all these Trusts the original owners or shareholders of the combined factories had to take up themselves a portion of the shares. These are not included in the tables given.

of the centralisation of capital, has, with a total capital of £1,300,000, 4,650 shareholders, of which only 550 possess a holding above £500.*

These are some examples of the splitting up of shares of property in centralised undertakings. Now, obviously, not all shareholders deserve the name of capitalists, and often one and the same great capitalist appears in all possible companies as a moderate shareholder. But with all this the number of shareholders and the average amount of their holding of shares has been of rapid growth. Altogether the number of shareholders in England is estimated at much more than a million, and that does not appear extravagant if one considers

---

* Rowntree and Sherwell, in *The Temperance Problem and Social Reform*, give the following list of the shareholders of five well-known British breweries :—

Breweries.	Shareholders of Ordinary Shares.	Pref. Shares.
Arthur Guinness, Son and Co....	5450	3768
Bass, Ratcliff and Gretton ...	17	1368
Threlfalls	577	872
Combe and Co.	10	1040
Samuel Alsopp and Co.	1313	2189
	7367	9237

Together, 16,604 shareholders of the whole £9,710,000 ordinary and preference stocks. Besides, the said companies had issued debentures to the amount of £6,110,000. If we assume a similar distribution of these, we would arrive at about 27,000 persons as co-proprietors of the five breweries. Now in 1898 the London Stock Exchange list enumerated more than 119 breweries and distilleries whose capital in circulated shares alone amounted to more than £70,000,000, apart from the fact that of sixty-seven of these companies the ordinary shares were as vendors' shares in private hands. All this points to whole armies of capitalists of every description in the brewing and distilling trades.

that in the year 1896 alone the number of
limited companies in the United Kingdom ran
to over 21,223, with a paid-up capital of
£1,145,000,000,* in which, moreover, the
foreign undertakings not negotiated in England
itself, the Government Stocks, etc., are not
included. †

This division of national wealth, for which
word in the great majority of cases one may
substitute national surplus value, is shown again
in the figures of the statistics of incomes.

In the United Kingdom in the financial year
1893-4 (the last return to my hand) the number
of persons with estimated incomes of £150 and
over, under Schedules D and E (incomes from
business profits, higher official posts, etc.)
amounted to 727,270.‡ But to that must still
be added those assessed on incomes taxed for
ground and land (rents, farm rents), for houses
let, taxable capital investments. These groups
together pay almost as much duty as the above-
named groups of taxpayers, namely, on 300
against 350 millions of pounds income.§ That
would nearly double the number of persons
referred to of over £150 income.

In the *British Review* of May 22nd, 1897,

---

* [The number in existence in April, 1907, was 43,038,
with a paid-up capital of £2,061,010,586.—ED.]

† In 1898 it was estimated that £2,150,000,000 of
English capital was invested abroad, and its yearly
increase was on an average £5,700,000. [In 1908, the
total was estimated at £3,000,000,000.—ED.]

‡ [In 1907 the number of persons with increases over
£160 was 894,249.—ED.]

§ [The figures for 1907 are £327,900,650 as against
£518,669,541.—ED.]

there are some figures on the growth of incomes
in England from 1851 to 1881. According to
those England contained in round numbers, in
1851, 300,000 families with incomes from £150
to £1,000 (the middle and lower bourgeoisie
and the highest aristocracy of labour) and
990,000 in 1881. Whilst the population in
these thirty years increased in the ratio of 27
to 35, that is about 30 per cent., the number of
families in receipt of these incomes increased in
the ratio of 27 to 90, that is 233⅓ per cent.
Giffen estimates to-day there are 1,500,000 of
these taxpayers.*

Other countries show no materially different
picture. France has, according to Mulhall,
with a total of 8,000,000 families, 1,700,000
families in the great and small bourgeois conditions of existence (an average income of
£260), against 6,000,000 of the working class
and 160,000 quite rich. In Prussia, in 1854, as
the readers of Lassalle know, with a population
of 16.3 millions, there were only 44,407 persons
with an income of over 1,000 thaler. In the
year 1894-5, with a total population of nearly
33,000,000, 321,296 persons paid taxes on incomes of over £150. In 1897-8 the number
had risen to 347,328. Whilst the population
doubled itself the class in better circumstances
increased more than sevenfold. Even if one
makes allowance for the fact that the provinces
annexed in 1866 show greater numbers of the

---

* [Mr. Chiozza Money estimates that in 1903-4 there
were 750,000 persons whose means were between £160
and £700 per annum.—ED.]

well-to-do than Old Prussia and that the prices of many articles of food had risen considerably in the interval, there is at least an increased ratio of the better-off to the total population of far more than two to one.* The conditions are precisely the same in the most industrial state of Germany, namely, Saxony. There from 1879 to 1894 the number of persons assessed for income tax was as follows :—

Income. £	1897	1894.	INCREASE Absolute.	Per cent.
Up to 40 ...	... 828686	... 972257	... 143571	... 17.3
40 to 80 ...	... 165362	... 357974	... 192612	... 116.4
Proletarian incomes	994048	...1330231	... 336183	... 33.8
80 to 165 ...	... 61810	... 106136	... 44326	... 71.6
165 to 480 ...	... 24072	... 41890	... 17818	... 74.0
480 to 2700 ...	... 4683	... 10518	... 5835	... 154.4
Over 2700 ...	... 238	... 886	... 648	... 272.0
Total ...	1084851	...1489661	... average	... 37.3

* The demonstrative value of the Prussian figures has been disputed on the ground that the principles of assessment had been considerably changed between 1854 and the end of the century. That this fact reduces their force of demonstration I have at once admitted. But let us take the figures of the Prussian income tax for 1892, the first year after the reform of taxation of 1891, and for 1907 where the same system ruled. There we get the following picture :—

Assessed Incomes. £	1892.	1907.	INCREASE Absolute.	Per cent.
150 to 300 ...	204714	... 387247	... 172533	... 84.3
300 to 1525 ...	103730	... 151574	... 47847	... 46.1
1525 to 5000 ...	6665	... 17109	... 10444	... 156.7
5000 and over ...	1,780	... 3,561	... 1,781	... 100.

The increase of the population was slightly over 20 per cent. We see the whole section of the well-to-do go on quicker than the population, and the quickest rate is not in the group of the high magnates, but in that of the simply easy classes. As far as fortunes are concerned, there were, in 1895 (the first year of the tax on fortunes), 13,600 with £25,000 and over ; in 1908 this number was in round figures 21,000, an increase of over 50 per cent. This shows how the capitalist clan grows.

The two capitalist classes, those with incomes above £480, show comparatively the greatest increase.

Similarly with the other separate German states. Of course, not all the recipients of higher incomes are " proprietors," *i.e.*, have unearned incomes ; but one sees that this is the case to a great extent because in Prussia for 1895-6, 1,152,332 persons with a taxable net amount of capital property of over £300 were drawn upon for the recruiting tax. Over half of them, namely, 598,063, paid taxes on a net property of more than £1,000, and 385,000 on one of over £1,600.

It is thus quite wrong to assume that the present development of society shows a relative or indeed absolute diminution of the number of the members of the possessing classes. Their number increases both relatively and absolutely. If the activity and the prospects of social democracy were dependent on the decrease of the " wealthy," then it might indeed lie down to sleep.* But the contrary is the case. The prospects of socialism depend not on the decrease but on the increase of social wealth.

Socialism, or the social movement of modern times, has already survived many a superstition, it will also survive this, that its future depends on the concentration of wealth or, if one will put it thus, on the absorption of surplus value by a diminishing group of capitalist mammoths.

---

* Karl Kautsky at the Stuttgart Congress of the German social democracy against the remark in my letter that the capitalists do increase and not decrease.

Whether the social surplus produce is accumulated in the shape of monopoly by 10,000 persons or is shared up in graduated amounts among half-a-million of men makes no difference in principle to the nine or ten million heads of families who are worsted by this transaction. Their struggle for a more just distribution or for an organisation which would include a more just distribution is not on that account less justifiable and necessary. On the contrary, it might cost less surplus labour to keep a few thousand privileged persons in sumptuousness than half-a-million or more in wealth.

If society were constituted or had developed in the manner the socialist theory has hitherto assumed, then certainly the economic collapse would be only a question of a short span of time. Far from society being simplified as to its divisions compared with earlier times, it has been graduated and differentiated both in respect of incomes and of business activities.

And if we had not before us the fact proved empirically by statistics of incomes and trades it could be demonstrated by purely deductive reasoning as the necessary consequence of modern economy.

What characterises the modern mode of production above all is the great increase in the productive power of labour. The result is a no less increase of production—the production of masses of commodities. Where are these riches? Or, in order to go direct to the heart of the matter: where is the surplus product that the industrial wage earners produce above their own consumption limited by their wages? If the " capitalist magnates " had ten times as large stomachs as popular satire attributes to them, and kept ten times as many servants as they really have, their consumption would only be a feather in the scale against the mass of yearly national product—for one must realise that the capitalist great industry means, above all, production of large quantities. It will be said that the surplus production is exported. Good, but the foreign customer also pays finally in goods only. In the commerce of the world the circulating metal, money, plays a diminishing rôle. The richer a country is in capital, the greater is its import of commodities, for the countries to which it lends money can as a rule only pay interest in the form of commodities.*

Where then is the quantity of commodities which the magnates and their servants do not consume? If they do not go in one way or another to the proletarians they must be caught up by other classes. Either a relatively growing decrease in the number of capitalists and an increasing wealth in the proletariat, or a numerous middle class—these are the only alternatives which the continued increase of production allows. Crises and unproductive expenses for armies, etc., devour much, but still they have latterly only absorbed a fractional part of the total surplus product. If the

---

* England receives its outstanding interest paid in the form of surplus imports to the value of £100,000,000 ; the greater part of which are articles of consumption.

working class waits till " Capital " has put the
middle classes out of the world it might really
have a long nap.   " Capital " would expropriate these classes in one form and then bring
them to life again in another.   It is not " Capital " but the working class itself which has the
task of absorbing the parasitic elements of the
social body.

As for the proposition in my letter to the
Stuttgart Congress that the increase of social
wealth is not accompanied by a diminishing
number of capitalist magnates but by an increasing number of capitalists of all degrees, a
leading article in the socialist New York *Volkszeitung* taxes me with its being false, at least,
as far as concerns America, for the census of
the United States proves that production there
is under the control of a number of concerns
" diminishing in proportion to its amount."
What a reputation !   The critic thinks he can
disprove what I assert of the division of the
classes by pointing to the divisions of industrial undertakings.   It is as though someone
said that the number of proletarians was
shrinking in modern society because where the
individual workman formerly stood the trade
union stands to-day.

Karl Kautsky also—at the time in Stuttgart
—took up the sentence just mentioned and
objected that if it were true that the capitalists
were increasing and not the propertyless classes,
then capitalism would be strengthened and we
socialists indeed should never attain our goal.
But the word of Marx is still true :" Increase of

capital means also increase of the proletariat."
That is the same confusion of issues in
another direction and less blunt. I had nowhere said that the proletarians did not increase.
I spoke of men and not of *entrepreneurs* when
I laid emphasis on the increase of capitalists.
But Kautsky evidently was captured by the
concept of "Capital," and thence deduced
that a relative increase of capitalists must
needs mean a relative decrease of the proletariat,
which would contradict our theory. And he
maintains against me the sentence of Marx
which I have quoted.

I have elsewhere quoted a proposition of
Marx* which runs somewhat different from the
one quoted by Kautsky. The mistake of
Kautsky lies in the identification of capital
with capitalists or possessors of wealth. But
I would like, besides, to refer Kautsky to something else which weakens his objection. And
that is what Marx calls the *organic* development
of capital. If the composition of capital
changes in such a way that the constant capital
increases and the variable decreases, then in the
businesses concerned the absolute increase of
capital means a relative decrease of the proletariat. But according to Marx that is just
the characteristic form of modern evolution.
Applied to capitalist economy as a whole, it
really means absolute increase of capital, relative decrease of the proletariat.

* *Capital*, I., chapter xxiii., par. 2, where it is said
that the number of capitalists grows "more or less"
through partitions of capital and offshoots of the same, a
fact later on left wholly out of account by Marx.

The workers who have become superabundant through the change in the organic composition of capital find work again each time only in proportion to the new capital on the market that can engage them.   So far as the point which Kautsky debates is concerned, my proposition is in harmony with Marx's theory.   If the number of workers increase, then capital must increase at a relatively quicker rate—that is the consequence of Marx's reasoning.   I think Kautsky will grant that without further demur.*

So far we are only concerned as to whether the increased capital is capitalist property only when employed by the undertaker or also when held as shares in an undertaking.

If not, the first locksmith Jones, who carries on his trade with six journeymen and a few apprentices would be a capitalist, but Smith, living on his private means, who has several hundred thousands of marks in a chest, or his son-in-law, the engineer Robinson, who has a greater number of shares which he received as a dowry (not all shareholders are idle men) would be members of the non-possessing class. The absurdity of such classification is patent. Property is property, whether fixed or personal. The share is not only capital, it is indeed capital in its most perfect, one might say its most refined, form.   It is the title to a share of the surplus product of the national or world-wide

---

* *Note to the English edition.*—I am sorry to say Kautsky did not frankly admit his error. He carped at the statistics I have adduced and replied finally that indeed the *idle* capitalists increased, as if I had represented the capitalist class as a class of workers.

economy freed from all gross contact with the pettinesses of trade activities—dynamic capital, if you like. And if they each and all lived only as idle *"rentiers,"* the increasing troops of shareholders—we can call them to-day armies of shareholders—even by their mere existence, the manner of their consumption, and the number of their social retainers, represent a most influential power over the economic life of society. The shareholder takes the graded place in the social scale which the captains of industry used to occupy before the concentration of businesses.

Meanwhile there is also something to be said about this concentration. Let us look at it more closely.

(c) *The Classes of Establishments in the Production and Distribution of Social Wealth.*

General statistics are wanting of the classes of enterprises in industry as regards England which is considered the most advanced of the European countries in capitalist production. They exist only for certain branches of production placed under the Factory Laws and for individual localities.

In the factories and workshops coming under the Factory Laws there were engaged, according to the Factory Inspector's report for 1896, altogether 4,398,983 persons.*   That is not

---

* [It would serve no good purpose to give more recent statistics, and it is impossible in some of the cases given

quite half the number given as actively engaged in industry according to the census of 1891. The number in the census, omitting the transport trade, is 9,025,902. Of the 4,626,919 remaining persons, we can reckon a fourth to a third as tradesmen in the branches of production referred to, and in some medium-sized and large businesses which do not come under the Factory Laws.

There remain in round numbers 3,000,000 employees and small masters in minute businesses. The 4,000,000 workers under the Factory Laws were distributed among 160,948 factories and workshops which yields an average of twenty-seven to twenty-eight workers per establishment.*

If we deal with factories and workshops separately we get 76,297 factories with 3,743,418 employees and 81,669 workshops with 655,565 employees, on the average forty-nine workers to a factory and eight to a registered workshop.

The average number of forty-nine workers to a factory already shows what the closer examination of the tables of the report confirms, that at least two-thirds of the businesses registered as factories belong to the category of

---

to follow exactly Mr. Bernstein's figures and so make accurate comparisons. Moreover, our Home Office does not now publish statistics compiled in the same way as in 1896.—Ed.]

* The particulars of 1,931 registered factories and 5,624 workshops had not come in when the report was drawn up. They would have somewhat diminished the ratio of workers to a business.

medium-sized businesses with six to fifty workers so that at the most 20,000 to 25,000 businesses of fifty workers and more remain which may represent, on the whole, about 3,000,000 workers. Of the 1,171,990 persons engaged in the transport trade only three-quarters can be considered at the most as belonging to large enterprises. If we add these to the foregoing categories we get a total for the workers and the auxiliaries of the large industries of between $3\frac{1}{2}$ and 4 millions, and against these stand $5\frac{1}{2}$ millions of persons engaged in medium and small businesses. The "workshop of the world" is, accordingly, far from being, as is thought, in the stage of containing only large industries. Enterprises show the greatest diversity in size also in the British Empire, and no class of any size disappears from the scale.*

If we compare with the above figures those of the German industrial census of 1895, we find that the latter, on the whole, shows the same picture as the English. The great industries occupied nearly the same position in relation to production in Germany in 1895 as in England in 1891. In Prussia in 1895, 38 per cent. of the industrial workers belonged to the large industries. The development of large undertakings has been accomplished there and in the rest of Germany with extraordinary speed. If

---

* German workmen who have emigrated to England have repeatedly expressed their astonishment to me at the dispersion of enterprises which they met in the wood, metal and manufacturing industries of this country. The present figures in the cotton industry show only a moderate increase in the concentration of establishments since the time when Karl Marx wrote.

certain branches of industry (among them the textile) are in this respect still behind England, others (machines and implements) have reached the English position on the average, and some (the chemical and glass industries and certain branches of the printing trades, and probably also electric engineering) have overtaken it. Still the great mass of persons engaged in industry belong also in Germany to small and medium undertakings. Of the $10\frac{1}{4}$ million persons engaged in industry in 1895 something over 3 millions were found in large undertakings, $2\frac{1}{2}$ millions in medium-sized undertakings (6 to 50 persons), and $4\frac{3}{4}$ millions in small ones. Master artisans still numbered $1\frac{1}{4}$ millions. In five trades their number, as against that of 1882, had increased absolutely and relatively (to the increase of population), in nine only absolutely, and in eleven it had declined absolutely and relatively.*

---

* See R. Calwer, "The Development of Handicraft," *Neue Zeit* xv., 2, p. 597.

The figures of the imperial census of 1907 are not yet known so far as the development in regard to size is concerned. But the figures for Prussia are known, and they can be taken as a fair average for the whole Empire. They show for trade respectively, industry and commerce together (without railways, post and telegraphs) the following figures :—

Establishments.	Numbers		Persons employed	
	1895.	1907.	1895.	1907.
Quite small (1 person only) ...	1,029,954	955,707	1 029,954	955,707
Small 2–5 persons)	593,884	767,200	1,638,205	2,038,236
Medium (6–50 persons)	108,800	154,330	1,390,745	2,109,164
Great (51–500 persons)	10,127	17,287	1.217,085	2,095,065
Very great (501–1,000 persons) ...	380	602	261,507	424,587
Giant (1,001 persons and over ...	191	371	338,585	710,253
	1,743,336	1,895,497	5,876,083	8,332,912

A remarkable movement towards the great establishments, and often two or more of the establishments

In France industry still keeps behind agriculture in numbers of workpeople employed. According to the census of April 17th, 1894, it represented only 25.9 per cent. of the population, and agriculture nearly twice as much—namely, 47.3 per cent. Austria shows a similar ratio, where agriculture takes 55.9 per cent. of the population and industry 25.9 per cent. In France there were one million persons working for themselves to 3.3 million employees, and in Austria 600,000 of the former to $2\frac{1}{4}$ million workmen and day labourers. Here the ratio is also very much the same. Both lands show a series of highly-developed industries (textile, mining, building, etc.), which, with respect to the size of the industry, compete with the most advanced countries, but which are only a portion of the industrial life-work of the nation.

Switzerland has, with 127,000 persons working for themselves, 400,000 employees. The United States of America, which the contributor to the New York *Volkszeitung* above referred to says is the most developed capitalist country in the world, certainly had, according to the census of 1890, a comparatively high average of workers per establishment—namely, $3\frac{1}{2}$ million workers to 355,415 industrial establishments, *i.e.,* 10 to 1. But the home and small industries are wanting here, just as in England.

---

enumerated are only departments of one and the same enterprise. The process of industrial and commercial concentration is most obvious. But that it does not mean the disappearance of the small enterprise is no less obvious. It is only the quite small enterprise—the garret workers, etc.—that as a group shows a decrease.

If one takes the figures of the Prussian industrial statistics from the top downwards, one gets almost exactly the same average as that of the American census. And if one studies more closely the *Statistical Abstract* of the United States, one comes upon a great number of manufacturing concerns with, on an average, five or fewer workers to the establishment. On the very first page we have 910 manufactories of agricultural implements with 30,723 workers, 35 ammunition factories with 1,993 workers, 251 manufactories of artificial feathers and flowers with 3,638, 59 manufactories of artificial limbs with 154, and 581 sail-cloth and awning factories with 2,873 workers.

If the continual improvement of technical methods and centralisation of businesses in an increasing number of branches of industry is a fact whose significance scarcely any crazy reactionaries can hide from themselves, it is a no less well-established fact that in a whole series of branches of industry small and medium-sized undertakings appear quite capable of existing beside the large industries. In industry there is no development according to a pattern that applies equally to one and all branches. Businesses carried on throughout according to routine, continue as small and medium-sized undertakings, whilst branches of technical trades which were thought to be secured for small businesses are absorbed for ever one fine day by a large organisation.

A whole series of circumstances allows the continuance and renewal of small and medium enterprises. They can be divided into three groups.

First, a great number of trades or branches of trades are nearly equally adapted for small and medium undertakings as for large enterprises, and the advantages which the latter have over the former are not so important that they can outweigh the peculiar advantages of the smaller home industries. This is, as everyone knows, the case, amongst others, with different branches of wood, leather, and metal work. Or, a division of labour is found where the large industry carries out one-half and three-quarters of the manufacture and when the finishing processes are done by smaller enterprises.

Secondly, when the product must be made accessible to the consumer, small establishments are, in many cases, favourable to its manufacture, as is shown most clearly in bakeries. If only the technical side was concerned, baking would long ago have been absorbed by the large industries, for the many bread factories yielding a good profit show that they can be carried on with good results. But in spite of, or beside, them and the cake factories which are gradually winning a market, the small and medium-sized bakeries hold their ground owing to the advantage they offer for trade with consumers in their vicinity. The master bakers are sure of their lives for some time to come as far as they have to reckon only with capitalist undertakings. Their increase since 1882 has certainly not kept step with the increase of population, but is still worth mentioning (77,609 as against 74,283).*

But baking is only an extreme example. For a whole series of trades—namely, where productive and service-performing labour are mixed—the same thing holds good. We will mention here the farrier and wheelwright trades. The American census shows 28,000 farrier and wheelwright businesses with a total of 50,867 persons, of which just one-half are masters. The German trade statistics show 62,722 blacksmiths and farriers; and it will certainly be a good while before the automatic vehicle driven by steam power, etc., will extinguish their spark of life in order to breathe life into new small workshops, as everyone knows bicycles have done. Similarly with the trades of tailors, shoemakers, saddlers, carpenters, carpetmakers, watchmakers, etc., where work for customers, and, in varying degree, repairing or shopkeeping, will keep alive independent existences of which certainly many, but not all, by any means, represent only proletarian incomes.

Last, but not least, the large industry itself gives life to smaller and medium trades partly by production on a large scale producing a corresponding cheapening of materials of work (auxiliary materials, half-manufactured goods), partly by the liberating of capital, on the one hand, and the "setting free" of workers on the other. In great and small amounts new capital is

---

* In Prussia the increase from 1895 to 1907 was from 52,045 to 62,985, over 20 per cent.; whilst the population increased only by 19 per cent.

always entering the market seeking utilisation, and the demand on the market for new goods increases steadily with the wealth of the community. Here the shareholders mentioned earlier play no small part. The market could not, in fact, live on the handful of millionaires even if the "hand" counted some thousand fingers. But the hundreds of thousands of rich and well-to-do have something to say to it. Nearly all the articles of luxury for these classes are, in the beginning—and very many also later on—manufactured in small and medium businesses, which, however, can also be capitalistic businesses, according as they work upon dear materials and use costly machines (manufacture of jewellery, work in fine metals, art embroidery). It is only later that the large industry (when it does not itself take over the articles referred to), by cheapening the materials of work, "democratises" the one or the other new luxury.

In spite of the continued changes in the grouping of industries and the internal organisation of the establishments, we have this picture on the whole to-day : that the large industry does not continuously absorb the smaller and medium industries, but that it is growing up beside them. Only the very small enterprises decline relatively and absolutely.* But as regards the small and medium industries they do increase, as is shown for Germany by the following figures for employees in trades :

* This is confirmed by the new Prussian statistics quoted in a former note.

	1882.	1895.	Increase Per cent.
Small businesses (1–5 persons)	2,457,950	3,056,318	24·3
Small medium businesses (6–10 persons)	500,097	833,409	66·6
Greater medium businesses (11–50 persons)	891,623	1,620,848	81·8

The population increased in the same period by 13.5 per cent. only.

Although in the interval treated the large industries increased their armies at a still greater rate—by 88.7 per cent—that has only meant in isolated cases the total absorption of the small businesses. In fact, in many cases no—or no more—competition takes place between large and small enterprises (think of the great works for making machinery and bridges). The example of the textile industry, which is commonly brought into our literature, is in many respects misleading. The increase of productivity which the mechanical mule represents over the old spindle has only recurred now and again. Very many large undertakings are superior to small or medium businesses, not on account of the higher productivity of the labour employed, but simply from the size of the undertaking (building of ships), and they leave the spheres of business of the small industries quite, or, to a great extent, untouched. He who hears that Prussia in the year 1895 saw nearly double as many workers occupied in large industries as in 1895; that these in 1882 were only 28.4 per cent., but in 1895 were 38 per cent. of the total number employed in all trades, might easily fancy that small industries would soon be a thing of the past, and that they had played their part in the social ecomony. The figures quoted show that the rapid extension and expansion of large industries represent only one side of social development.

As in industry so in commerce. In spite of the shooting up of the large warehouses the medium and small commercial businesses maintain their footing. We are, of course, not concerned here with denying the parasitic element in commerce, particularly as regards the so-called small retail business. Nevertheless, it must be observed that also with regard to that, much exaggeration has crept in. Wholesale production and the steadily increasing intercourse all over the world are always throwing greater quantities of commodities on the market which in some way or other must be brought to the consumer. Who would deny that this could take place with less expenditure of labour and cost than by the present retail trade? But as long as it does not take place this kind of trade will persist. And just as it is an illusion to expect from the large industries that they will absorb in a short time the small and medium industries, so is it also Utopian to expect from the capitalistic warehouses an absorption to a considerable extent of medium-sized and small shops. They injure individual businesses and here and there temporarily bring the whole of the small trades into confusion. But after a time the latter find a way of competing with the large shops and of making use of all the advantages which local associations offer them. Fresh specialising and fresh combining of businesses are begun, new forms and methods of carrying on business are started.

The capitalistic warehouse is far oftener a product of the great increase of the abundance of goods than an implement of the annihilation of a parasitic small trade. It has had more effect in rousing the latter from its routine and breaking it of certain monopolist customs than in exterminating it.

The number of shop businesses increases steadily; it rose in England between 1875 and 1886 from 295,000 to 366,000. The number of persons employed in commerce rose still more. As the English statistics under this heading were taken on a different basis from those of 1881,* we will take the figures from the Prussian statistics.

There were in Prussia in shops and carrying trades (excluding railways and post office business) :—

	1885.	1895.	Increase Per cent.
In businesses with 2 and fewer assistants	411,509	467,656	13·6
„ „ 3–5 assistants	176,867	342,112	93·4
„ „ 6–50 „	157,328	303,078	92·6
„ „ 51 assistants and more	25,619	62,056	142·2
	771,323	1,174,902	

The increase is proportionately the greatest in the large businesses, but these do not represent much more than 5 per cent. of the whole. It is not the large businesses that offer the most deadly competition to the small ones; the latter provide it among themselves. But in proportion there are not very many corpses. And the scale of businesses remains unhurt in its composition.

---

* As far as appears from them, they show an increase of over 50 per cent. in the last decade.

The small medium-sized shops show the greatest increase.

Finally, when we come to agriculture, as far as concerns the size of separate undertakings, we meet, in our times, with a movement all over Europe, and partially in America, which apparently contradicts everything that the socialistic theory has hitherto advanced. Industry and commerce showed only a slower movement upwards in large undertakings than was assumed, but agriculture shows a standing-still or a direct retrogression in regard to the size of holdings.

As regards Germany, the census of occupations taken in 1895, as against 1882, shows the relatively greatest increase in the group of peasant medium-sized holdings (5 to 20 hectares)—namely, 8 per cent.—and still greater is the increase in the area covered by the whole of them—namely, 9 per cent. The peasants' small holdings following next below them (2 to 5 hectares) show the next greatest increase : 3.5 per cent. increase in the number of holdings and 8 per cent. increase in extent of land held. The very small holdings (allotments) (under 2 hectares) have an increase of 5.8 per cent. in number and 12 per cent. in land occupied, yet the portion of this land used for agricultural purposes shows a diminution of 1 per cent. The holdings already partially capitalistic (20 to 100 hectares) show an increase of not quite 1 per cent., which falls to the land cultivated as forest, and an increase of not quite ⅓ per cent. is shown by the large holdings (more than 100 hectares).

Here are the figures referred to for 1895 :—

Kind of Holding.	No. of Holdings.	No. of hectares used for agricultural purposes.	Total extent in hectares.
Very small (2 hectares and under) ...	3,236,367	1,808,444	2,415,414
Small peasants' holdings (2-5 hectares)	1,016,318	3,285,984	4,142,071
Medium „ „ (5-20 hectares)	998,804	9,721,875	12,537,660
Large „ „ (20-100 hectares)	281,767	9,869,837	13,157,201
Large holdings (100 hectares & upwards)	25,061	7,831,801	11,031,896

Over two-thirds of the total area fall under the three categories of peasant farms, about one-third under large holdings. In Prussia the proportion of peasant holdings is even more favourable; they occupy nearly three-fourths of the agricultural area—22,875,000 out of 32,591,000 hectares.

If we turn from Prussia to its neighbour, Holland, we find :—

Area of Holding.	Holdings 1884.	1893.	Increase or decrease.	Per cent.
1-5 hectares ...	66,842	777,767	+10,925	+16·2
5-10 „ ...	31,552	34,199	+2,647	+8·4
10-50 „ ...	48,278	51,940	+3,662	+7·6
Over 50 hectares	3,554	3,510	—44	—1·2

Here the large holdings have actually decreased and the small medium peasants' holdings have considerably increased.*

In Belgium, according to Vandervelde,† the ownership of the land as well as the occupation of the soil has yielded to a continued decentralisation. The last general statistics show an increase of owners of land from 201,226 in the year 1846 to 293,524 in the year 1880; an increase also of tenants of land from 371,320 to 616,872. The total cultivated agricultural area of Belgium consisted in 1880 of not quite

---

* See W. H. Vliejen : *Das Agrarprogramm der niederländischen Sozialdemokratie, Neue Zeit* xvii., 1, p. 75.

† *Der Agrasozialismus in Belgien, Neue Zeit* xv. 1, p. 752.

2,000,000 hectares, of which over one-third were cultivated by their owners. The division of agricultural allotments reminds one of the Chinese agrarian conditions.

France in the year 1882 had the following agricultural holdings :—

		Holdings.	Extent of Holding.
Under 1 hectare	...	2,167,767	1,083,833 hectares
1–10 hectares	...	2,635,030	11,366,274 „
10–40 „	...	727,088	14,845,650 „
40–100 „	...	113,285	
100–200 „	...	20,644	22,266,104 „
200–500 „	...	7,942	
Over 500 „	...	217	

Of the holdings between 40 and 100 hectares there are in round numbers 14 million hectares, and of those over 200 hectares 8,000,000, so that, on the whole, the large holdings represent between a fifth and a sixth of the agriculturally-cultivated area. The smaller, medium, and large peasants' holdings cover nearly three-quarters of French soil. From 1862 to 1882 the holdings of 5 to 10 hectares had increased by 24 per cent; those between 10 and 40 acres by 14.28 per cent. The agricultural statistics of 1892 show an increase of the total number of holdings of 30,000, but a decrease in the last-named category of 33,000, which shows a further sub-division of holdings of land.

But how does it stand in England, the classic land of large ownerships of land and of capitalistic farming of the soil? We know the lists of mammoth landlords which from time to time appear in the press as an illustration of the concentration in the ownership of land in England, and we know the passage in *Capital* where Marx says that the assertion of John Bright that 150 landlords own the half of British land and 12 the half of Scottish, has not been denied.* Now, though the land of England is centralised by monopolists, it is not so to the extent that John Bright pronounced. According to Brodrick's *English Land and English Landlords* there were out of the 33 millions of acres of land in England and Wales entered in Domesday Book, 14 millions, in round numbers, the property of 1,704 landlords with 3,000 acres each or more. The remaining 19 million acres were divided among 150,000 owners of one acre and more, and a large number of owners of small plots of land. Mulhall gave, in 1892, for the whole of the United Kingdom, 176,520 as the number of owners of more than 10 acres of land (altogether ten-elevenths of the area). How is this soil cultivated? Here are the figures of 1885 and 1895 for Great Britain (England, with Wales and Scotland, but without Ireland), changed into hectares for the sake of more convenient comparison.† These were enumerated :—

Holdings.			1885.	1895.	Increase or decrease.
2–20 hectares	...	...	232,955	235,481	+2,526
20–40 „	...	...	64,715	66,625	+1,910
40–120 „	...	...	79,573	81,245	+1,672
120–200 „	...	...	13,875	13,568	+307
Over 200 „	...	...	5,489	5,219	—270

Here, too, is a decrease of the large and the very large holdings and an increase of the small and medium-sized ones.

The figures, nevertheless, tell us nothing of

---

* *Capital*, I., 4th ed., p. 615.

† According to the ratio of 1 acre = 40 acres, which is not quite exact, but which appears admissible for the purpose of comparison. The numbers are taken from the Blue Book on Agricultural Holdings.

the cultivated area. Let us complete them by
the figures of the different areas coming under
the various classes of holdings. They make a
positively bewildering picture. There were in
Great Britain in 1895 :—

	Acres.	Percentage of Total area.
Holdings under 2 hectares* ...	366,792	1·13
Holdings of 2-5 ,, ...	1,667,647	5·12
,, 5-20 ,. ...	2,864,976	8·74
,, 20-40 ,, ...	4,885,203	15·0
,, 40-120 ,, ...	13,875,914	42·59
,, 120-200 ,, ...	5,113,945	15·7
,, 200-400 ,, ...	3,001,184	9·42
,, over 400 ,, ...	801,852	2·46

According to this 27 to 28 per cent. of the agricultural land of Great Britain is in large holdings, and only 2.46 per cent. is in very large
holdings. On the other hand, over 66 per cent.
is in medium and large peasants' holdings.
The proportion of the peasant holdings (where,
nevertheless, capitalistic large peasant holdings
predominate) is greater in England than in the
average in Germany. Even in England proper
the holdings between 5 and 120 hectares com-
prise 64 per cent. of the cultivated area, and
nearly 13 per cent. of the area only is in holdings
of over 200 hectares.* In Wales, quite apart
from small allotments, 92 per cent., in Scotland
72 per cent. of the holdings are peasant holdings
of between 2 and 100 hectares.

Of the cultivated area, 61,014 holdings with

---

* Of which 579,133 plots come under 1 acre.

† [In 1907, 21.78 of all holdings in England were
between 1 and 5 acres, and only 3.95 holdings were over
300 acres. The same figures for Wales were 16.91 and
0.66 ; for Scotland 22.40 and 3.66.—Ed.]

4.6 millions of acres of land were the property
of their cultivators, 19,607 holdings were partly
the property and partly leased, and 439,405
holdings only were on leased land. It is well
known that in Ireland the small peasant class or
small tenant class predominates. The same
holds good for Italy.

There can, then, be no doubt that in the whole
of Western Europe, as also in the Eastern
States of the United States, the small and
medium agricultural holding is increasing everywhere, and the large and very large holding
is decreasing. There is no doubt that the
medium holdings are often of a pronounced
capitalistic type. The concentration of the
enterprises is not accomplished here in the form
of annexing an ever greater portion of land to
the farm, as Marx saw in his time,* but actually
in the form of intensification of the cultivation,
changes in cultivation that need more labour
for a given area, or in the rearing, etc., of
superior cattle. It is well known that this is to
a large extent (not altogether) the result of the
competition between the agricultural states or
agricultural territories of Eastern Europe and
those over the seas. Also these latter will be
in a position for a good while yet to produce
corn and a number of other products of the soil
at such cheap prices that a substantial dis-
arrangement of the factors of development is
not to be expected from a change in this
respect.

---

* See *Capital*, I., 4th ed., p. 643, note.

Although the tables of statistics of income in the most advanced industrial countries may partly register the mobility, and with it the transitoriness and insecurity, of capital in modern economy, and although the incomes or fortunes registered may be to an increasing extent paper possessions which a vigorous puff of wind could indeed easily blow away; yet these rows of incomes stand in no fundamental opposition to the gradation of economic unities in industry, commerce, and agriculture. The scale of incomes and the scale of establishments show a fairly well-marked parallelism in their divisions, especially where the middle divisions are concerned. We see these decreasing nowhere, but, on the contrary, considerably increasing everywhere. What is taken away from them from above in one place they supplement from below in another, and they receive compensation from above in one place for that which falls from their ranks below. If the collapse of modern society depends on the disappearance of the middle ranks between the apex and the base of the social pyramid, if it is dependent upon the absorption of these middle classes by the extremes above and below them, then its realisation is no nearer in England, France, and Germany to-day than at any earlier time in the nineteenth century.

But a building can appear outwardly unchanged and substantial and yet be decayed if the stones themselves or important layers of stones have become rotten. The soundness of a business house stands the test of critical

periods ; it remains, therefore, for us to investigate what is the course of the economic crises
which are peculiar to the modern order of production, and what consequences and reactions
are to be expected in the near future from them.

(d) The Crises and Possibilities of Adjust-
ment in Modern Economy.

" The contradictions inherent in the movement of capitalist society impress themselves
upon the practical bourgeoisie most strikingly
in the changes of the periodic cycle through
which modern industry runs, and whose
crowning point is the universal crisis."—
MARX, Preface to the second edition of
Capital.

In Socialist circles the most popular explanation of economic crises is their derivation from
under-consumption. Friedrich Engels, however, has on several occasions combated this
idea sharply—most sharply, probably, in the
third part of the third chapter of the polemical
treatise against Dühring, where Engels says
that under-consumption by the masses may well
be "also a condition of crises," but that it
explains their presence to-day just as little as
their former absence. Engels illustrates this
by the conditions of the English cotton industry
in the year 1877, and declares it to be a strong
measure in the face of those conditions "to
explain the present total stagnation in the sale
of cotton yarns and textile fabrics by the under-
consumption of the English masses and not by

the over-production of the English cotton manufacturers."*

But Marx himself has also occasionally pronounced very sharply against the derivation of
crises from under-consumption. "It is pure
tautology," he writes in the second volume of
Capital, "to say that crises rise from a want of
consumers able to pay." If one wished to give
this tautology an appearance of greater reality
by saying that the working classes receive too
small a portion of what they produce, and that
the grievance would therefore be redressed if
they had a larger share, it can only be observed
that "the crises are each time preceded by a
period in which the workers' wages rise and the
working classes actually receive a relatively
greater share than usual of the yearly produce
destined for consumption." It thus would
appear that capitalist production "includes
conditions independent of good or evil inten-
tions—conditions which only permit of temporarily relative prosperity for the working classes
and then always as a stormy bird of a crisis."†
To which Engels adds in a footnote: "*Ad
notam* for the adherents of Rodbertus' theory
of crises."

A passage in the second part of the third

---

* Third edition, pp. 308, 309. [In a footnote to this
Engels remarks: "The explanation of crises by under-
consumption originated with Sismondi, and had with him
a certain justification." "Rodbertus," he says, "borrowed it from Sismondi and Dühring copied it from
him." In the preface to the *Poverty of Philosophy*
Engels also argues in similar fashion against the theory
of crises put forth by Rodbertus.]

† *Ibid.*, pp. 406, 407.

volume of *Capital* stands in apparent contradiction to all these statements. There Marx says about crises : " The last reason for all social crises always is the poverty and limitation of consumption of the masses as opposed to the impulse of capitalist production to develop the productive forces, as though only the absolute capacity for consumption of the community formed their limit.''* That is not very different from the Rodbertus' theory of crises, for with him also crises are not occasioned simply by under-consumption by the masses, but, just as explained here, by it in conjunction with the increasing productivity of labour. In the passage quoted by Marx, under-consumption of the masses is emphasised even in contradistinction to the anarchy of production—disparity of production in the various branches and changes of prices which produce temporarily general depressions—as the last reason of all true crises.

As for any real difference of conception appearing here from that expressed in the quotation given above from the second volume, an explanation must be sought in the very different times in which the two sentences were written. There is an interval of between thirteen to fourteen years between them, and the passage from the third volume of *Capital* is the earlier one. It was written by 1864 or 1865, whilst the one out of the second volume must have been written about 1878.† In another

---

* *Ibid.*, p. 21.

† Compare for this the statement of Engels in the preface to the second volume of *Capital*. Generally

passage of this second volume, which had been written by 1870, the periodic character of crises —which is approximately a ten-year cycle of production—is brought into conjunction with the length of the turnover of fixed (laid out in machinery, etc.) capital. The development of capitalistic production has a tendency on the one hand to extend the bulk of value and the length of life of fixed capital, and on the other to diminish this life by a constant revolution of the means of production. Hence the "moral wearing out" of this portion of fixed capital before it is "physically spent." Through this cycle of connected turnovers comprehending a series of years in which capital is confined through its fixed portion, arises a material cause for periodic crises in which the business passes through periods following one another of exhaustion, medium activity, precipitancy, crisis.* The periods for which capital is invested are certainly very diverse and do not coincide, but the crisis always forms the starting point of a great fresh investment and therewith—from the standpoint of the whole community—a more or less new material foundation for the next cycle.† This thought is taken up again in the same volume in the chapters on the reproduction of capital, and it is there shown how even with reproduction on the same scale and with unchanged productivity of labour, differences in

---

speaking the second volume contains the latest and ripest results of Marx's work of research.

* Vol. II., p. 164.

† P. 165.

the length of life of the fixed capital which
appear temporarily (if, for example, in one year
more constituent portions of fixed capital decay
than in the previous year) must have as a consequence crises of production. Foreign trade
can indeed help out, but so far as it does not
remove these differences it only transfers "the
conflicts to a wider sphere and opens to them a
greater scope." A communistic society could
prevent such disturbances by continued relative
over-production which in its case would be
" only the control of the community over its
own means of production "; but in a capitalistic
society this over-production is an anarchical
element. This example of disturbances merely
through the differences of length of life of
fixed capital is striking. Want of proportion
in the production of fixed and circulating capital
is one of the favourite arguments of the economists for explaining crises. It is something
quite new to them to hear that such a want of
proportion can and must arise from the simple
maintenance of fixed capital; that it can and
must arise with the assumption of an ideal
normal production and the simple reproduction
of the social capital already in use.* In the
chapter on "Accumulation and Reproduction on
a larger scale," over-production and crises are
only mentioned cursorily as self-evident results
of possibilities of combination which follow from
the process depicted. Yet here again the idea
of " over-production " is very vigorously maintained. " If," we find on page 499, " Fullarton,

* *Ibid.*, p. 468.

for example, will know nothing of over-produc-tion in the ordinary meaning of the term, but only of the over-production of capital—that is, pecuniary capital—that only shows again how very little even the best bourgeois economists understand the mechanism of their system." And on page 524 it is shown that if, as can occasionally happen even with capitalistic accumulation, the constant part of the portion of capital destined for the production of the means of consumption, is greater than wages capital plus the surplus value derived from the portion of capital destined for the creation of the means of production, this would be over-production in the former sphere and "would only be adjusted by a great commercial crash."

The thought above developed, that the open-ing out of markets would extend the conflicts of capitalistic economy to wider spheres, and therefore increase them, is in the third volume applied by Engels on different occasions to the newer phenomena. The notes on page 97 in the first part of this volume, and on page 17 in the second part, are much the most worthy of notice. In the latter note, which recapitulates and completes what is writen in the former, he mentions the enormous extension, since the time when Marx wrote, of the means of traffic, which has really made the whole world a market, particularly the entry of ever fresh industrial countries into competition with England, and the unlimited extension of the region for the investment of surplus European capital. All these are, according to him, factors which have

set aside or greatly weakened "most of the old
incubators of crises and opportunities for the
formation of crises." But after characterising
the Kartels and Trusts as a means for limiting
competition in the inner market, and the protective duties with which the non-English world
surrounds itself, as "armour for the final, universal industrial campaign which is to decide
the government of the world market," he ends :
"Thus each of the elements which strives
against a repetition of the old crises conceals in
itself the seed of a more powerful future crisis."
Engels raises the question whether the industrial cycle which in the infancy of world-wide
commerce (1815-1847) used to last about five
years, and from 1847 to 1867 ten years, has not
undergone a new extension, and whether we do
not "find ourselves in the preparatory period
of a new world-crash of unheard-of violence ";
but he also leaves this alternative open, that the
acute form of the periodic process with its
hitherto ten-year cycle may have yielded to a
"more chronic rotation allotted to different
lands at different times of relatively shorter,
feebler improvement of trade, with a relatively
long, indecisive depression."

The time that has elapsed since this was
written has left the question unanswered. Signs
of an economic world-wide crash of unheard-of
violence have not been established, nor can one
describe the improvement of trade in the intervals between the crises as particularly short-
lived. Much more does a third question arise
which after all is partly contained already in

the second—namely : (1) whether the enormous extension of the world market, in conjunction with the extraordinary shortening of time necessary for the transmission of news and for the transport trade, has so increased the possibilities of adjustment of disturbances; and (2) whether the enormously increased wealth of the European states, in conjunction with the elasticity of the modern credit system and the rise of industrial Kartels, has so limited the reacting force of local or individual disturbances that, at least for some time, general commercial crises similar to the earlier ones are to be regarded as improbable.

This question, raised by me in an essay on the " Socialist Theory of a Catastrophic Development of Society," has experienced all kinds of opposition.* Among others it has caused Rosa Luxemburg to lecture me in a series of articles published in the *Leipzig Volkszeitung* of September, 1898, on the nature of credit and the possibilities of capitalism in regard to adaptation. As these articles, which have also

---

* The essay criticised the opinion laid down in a resolution of the International Socialist Congress of 1896 that we were on the eve of a great catastrophic crisis that would produce a total revolution of social conditions. The said resolution ran thus : "The economic and industrial development is going on with such rapidity that a crisis may occur within a comparatively short time. The Congress, therefore, impresses upon the proletariat of all countries the imperative necessity of learning, as class-conscious citizens, how to administer the business of their respective countries for the common good." I gladly recognised the usefulness of the final recommendation, but I boldly disputed the truth of the premise. This occasioned some violent attacks, to which I replied in the letter reprinted in the preface of this book.

passed into other socialist papers, are true examples of false dialectics, but handled at the same time with great skill, it appears to me to be opportune to examine them here.

Rosa Luxemburg maintains that the credit system, far from working against crises, is the means of pushing them to an extremity. It first made possible the unmeasured extension of capitalistic production, the acceleration of the exchange of goods and of the cyclic course of the process of production, and in this way it is the means of bringing into active conflict as often as possible the differences between production and consumption. It puts into the hand of the capitalist the disposal of the capital of others, and with it the means of foolhardy speculation, and if depression sets in it intensifies the crisis. Its function is to banish the residue of stability from all capitalist conditions, to make all capitalist forces in the highest degree elastic, relative, and sensitive.

Now all that is not exactly new to anyone who knows a little of the literature of socialism in general and of Marxist socialism in particular. The only question is whether it rightly represents the real facts of the case to-day, or whether the picture has not another side. According to the laws of dialectic evolution to which Rosa Luxemburg so much likes to give play, it ought certainly to be the case ; but even without falling back upon these, one should realise that a thing like credit, capable of so many forms, must under different conditions work in different ways. Marx treats credit by no means from the point of view that it is only a destructive agent in the capitalist system. He assigns to it, amongst other things,* the function of " creating the form of transition to a new modus of production," and with regard to it he expressly brings into prominence " the double-sided characteristics of the credit system." Frau Luxemburg knows the passage referred to very well; she even reprints the sentence from it where Marx speaks of the mixed character, "half swindler, half prophet," of the chief promulgators of credit (John Law, Isaac Pereire, etc.). But she refers exclusively to the destructive side of the credit system, and mentions not a word of its capacity for establishing and creating, which Marx expressly includes. Why this amputation, why this noteworthy silence with respect to the "double-sided characteristics"? The brilliant dialectical fireworks by means of which the power of the credit system is represented as a means of adaptation in the light of a " one-day fly," end in smoke and mist as soon as one looks more closely at this other side which Frau Luxemburg passes by so shyly.

That the credit system makes speculation easier is an experience centuries old; and very old, too, is the experience that speculation does not stop production when industrial circumstances are far enough developed to suit it. Meanwhile, speculation is conditioned by the relation of the knowable to the unknown circumstances. The more the latter predominate

* Vol. III., i., p. 429.

the more will speculation flourish ; the more it is
restrained by the former, the more the ground is
cut from under its feet. Therefore the maddest
outbursts of commercial speculation come to
pass at the dawn of the capitalistic era, and
speculation celebrates its wildest orgies usually
in the countries where the capitalistic development is youngest. In the domain of industry
speculation flourished most luxuriantly in new
branches of production. The older a branch
of production is under modern forms—with the
exception of the manufacture of mere articles
of fashion—the more does the speculative
momentum cease to play a decisive part in it.
The conditions and movements of the market
are then more exactly foreseen and are taken
into consideration with greater certainty.

Nevertheless, this certainty is only relative,
because competition and technical development
exclude an absolute control of the market.
Over-production is to a certain extent unavoidable. But over-production in single industries
does not mean general crises. If it leads to
such an one, either the industries concerned must
be of such importance as consumers of the
manufactures of other industries, as that their
stagnation also stops these industries, or indeed
they must take from them, through the medium
of the money market—that is, through the
paralysis of general credit—the means of
carrying on production. But it is evident
that there is always a lessening probability of
this latter result. The richer a country is, the
more developed its credit organisation—which

is not to be confused with a more widely spread habit to produce with borrowed capital. For here the possibilities of adjustment multiply in an increasing measure. In some passage, which I cannot find at the moment, Marx said once—and the correctness of the sentence can be proved by the most abundant evidence—that the contractions in the centre of the money market are much more quickly overcome than in the different points of the circumference. But the change of the means of communication brought about in the meantime has more than neutralised the consequences of great distances in this respect.*

If the crises of the money market are not quite banished from the world yet, as far as concerns us here, the tightenings of that market by vast commercial undertakings controlled with difficulty are very much reduced.

The relations of financial crises to trade and business crises are not yet so fully explained that one can say with any certainty when both happen together that it was the trade crisis—

---

* Engels calculates that America and India have been brought nearer to the industrial countries of Europe, by means of the Suez Canal, steamer transport, etc., by 70 to 90 per cent., and adds "that owing to this the two great incubators of crises from 1825 to 1857 lost a great part of their destructive power" (*Capital*, Vol. III., Part I., p. 45). On p. 395 of the same volume, Engels maintains that certain speculative business formed on risky schemes of credit, which Marx pictures as factors of crises in the money market, have been brought to an end through the oceanic cable. The correcting parenthesis of Engels on p. 56 of the second part of Vol. III. is also worthy of notice for its criticism on the development of the credit system.

i.e., over-production—which directly caused the money crisis. In most cases it was quite clear that it was not actual over-production, but over-speculation, which paralysed the money market, and by this depressed the whole business. That is proved from the isolated facts which Marx mentions in the third volume of *Capital*, taken from the official inquiries into the crises of 1847 and 1857, as well as from the facts which Professor Herkner adduces on these and other crises in his sketch of the history of trade crises in his *Handwörterbuch der Staatswissenschaften*. Frau Luxemburg deduces on the basis of the facts adduced by Herkner that the crises hitherto have not at all been the right crises, but that they were only infantile illnesses of the capitalistic economy, the accompanying phenomena not of narrowing but of widening the domain of the capitalistic economy—that we "have not yet entered upon that phase of perfect capitalistic maturity which is presumed in the Marxist scheme of the periodicity of crises." According to her we find ourselves " in a phase where crises no longer accompany the rise of capital nor yet its decline." This time will only come when the world market is fully developed and can be enlarged by no sudden extensions. Then the struggle between the productive powers and the limits of exchange will become continually sharper and more stormy.

To that one must observe that the formula of the crises in and for Marx was no picture of the future, but a picture of the present day which it was expected would recur in the future in always sharper forms and in greater acuteness. As soon as Frau Luxemburg denies to it the significance which Marx imputed to it for the whole epoch lying behind us, and sets it up as a deduction which did not yet correspond with reality, but was only a logical forecast based on the existence of certain elements in an embryonic state, she immediately questions the whole Marxist prediction of the coming social evolution, so far as this is based on the theory of crises. For if this was not based on experience at the time when it was set up, and has not become manifest in the interval between then and now, in what more distant future can one place its formula as coming true? Its relegation to the time when the world market has been fully developed is a flight into the next world.

No one knows when the world market will be fully developed. Frau Luxemburg is not ignorant of the fact that there is an intensive as well as an extensive broadening of the world market, and that the former is to-day of much greater importance than the latter.

In the trade statistics of the great industrial countries exports play by far the greatest part in regard to the countries longest occupied. England exports to the whole of Australasia (all the Australian colonies, New Zealand, etc.) values less in amount than to a single country, France; to the whole of British North America (Canada, British Columbia, etc.) not so much as to Russia only; to both colonial territories together, which are indeed of a respectable age, not so much as to Germany. Its trade with all

its colonies, including the whole of the immense
Indian Empire, is not a third of its trade with
the rest of the world; and as regards the
colonial acquisitions of the last twenty years,
the exports thither have been ridiculously small.
The extensive widenings of the world market
are accomplished much too slowly to allow
sufficient outlet for the actual increase of
production, if the countries already drawn into
it did not offer it an increasing market. A limit
to this increasing and intensive amplifying of
the world market, along with the extension of its
area, cannot be set up *à priori*. If the universal
crisis is the inherent law of capitalistic production, it must prove its reality now or in the near
future. Otherwise the proof of its inevitableness hovers in the air of abstract speculation.

We have seen that the credit system to-day
undergoes less, not more, contractions leading
to the general paralysis of production, and so
far, therefore, takes a minor place as a factor
in forming crises. But so far as it is a means
of a hothouse forcing of over-production, the
associations of manufacturers meet this inflation
of production in separate countries, and even
internationally here and there, ever more
frequently, by trying to regulate production
as a Kartel, a syndicate, or a trust. Without
embarking in prophecies as to its final power of
life and work, I have recognised its capacity to
influence the relation of productive activity to
the condition of the market so far as to diminish
the danger of crises. Frau Luxemburg refutes
this also.

First she denies that the association of manufacturers can be general. She says the final aim and effect of such associations are, by excluding competition within a branch, to increase their share of the total amount of profit gained in the market of commodities. But, she adds, one branch of industry could only attain this at the cost of another, and the organisation could not possibly, therefore, be general. "Extended into all branches of production it would itself put an end to its effect."

This proof does not differ by a hair's-breadth from the proof, long ago abandoned, of the uselessness of trades unions. Its support is even immeasurably more fragile than the wages fund theory of blessed memory. It is the presumption unproven, unprovable, or, rather, proved to be false, that in the commodity market only a fixed amount of profit is to be divided. It presumes, amongst other things, a fixing of prices independently of the movements in the cost of production. But even given a fixed price, and, moreover, a fixed technological basis of production, the amount of profit in a branch of industry can be raised without thereby lessening the profits of another—namely, by the lessening of unproductive expenses, the ceasing of cutting competition, better organisation of production, and the like. That the association of manufacturers is an effective means towards this is self-evident. The problem of the division of profits is the last obstacle of all which stands in the way of a general union of associations of employers.

It stands somewhat better with the last objection of Frau Luxemburg. According to it the Kartels are unsuitable for preventing the anarchy of production because the Kartels of manufacturers as a rule obtain their higher profit rate on the home market, because they use the portion of capital that cannot be applied to this for manufacturing products for foreign countries at a much less profit rate. The consequence is, increased anarchy on the world market—the opposite to the object aimed at.

"As a rule" this manœuvre can only be upheld where a protective duty affords the Kartel protection, so as to make it impossible for the foreign country to repay it in like coin. Meanwhile we are concerned here neither with denying the harmful effects of the present simple and high protectionist system, nor with an apology for the syndicates of manufacturers. It has not occurred to me to maintain that Kartels, etc., are the last word of economic development, and are suited to remove for ever the contradictions of modern industrial life. I am, on the contrary, convinced that where in modern industrial countries Kartels and trusts are supported and strengthened by protective duties, they must, in fact, become factors of the crises in the industry concerned—also, if not at first, in any case finally, for the "protected" land itself. The question only arises how long the people concerned will be content with this arrangement. Protective tariffs are in themselves no product of economy, but an encroachment on economy by the political power seeking to secure

economic results. It is otherwise with the
industrial Kartel. It has—although favoured
by protective tariffs—grown out of the economic
soil, and is a national means of adapting
production to the movements of the market.
That it is, or can be, at the same time the means
of monopolist exploitation is another matter.
But it is just as much beside the question
that in the former capacity it means an increase
of all earlier remedial measures for over-
production. With much less risk than the
individual undertaking, it can, in times of
a glut on the market, temporarily limit
production. Better than this, it is also in a
position to meet foreign cutting competition
abroad. To deny this is to deny the superiority
of organisation over anarchic competition. But
we do so, if we deny on principle that Kartels
can work as a modifying influence on the nature
and frequency of crises. How *far* they can do
so is for the present a matter for conjecture, for
we have not sufficient experience to allow of a
conclusive judgment in this respect. But still
fewer conclusive facts can be given under these
circumstances for anticipating future general
crises as they hovered before Marx and Engels,
repetitions on a larger scale of the crises of 1825,
1836, 1847, 1857, 1873. The mere fact that whilst
for a long time socialists generally believed in
an increasing contraction of the industrial cycle
as the natural consequence of the increasing
concentration of capital—a development in the
form of a spiral—Friedrich Engels in 1894
found himself driven to question whether a new

enlarging of the cycle was not in front of us, and thus to suggest the exact contrary of the former assumption, and he warned us against the abstract deduction that these crises must repeat themselves in the old form.*

The history of individual industries shows that their crises by no means always coincide with the so-called general crises. Marx, as we have seen, believed he could establish on the need of an accelerated renewal of fixed capital (implements of production, etc.) a material foundation for periodic crises,† and it is undoubtedly true that an important reason for crises is to be found here. But it is not accurate, or not more accurate, that these periods of renewal coincide as to time in the various industries. And therewith a further factor of the great general crisis is done away with.

There remains then only so much, that the capacity for production in modern society is much greater than the actual demand for products determined by the buying capacity; that millions live insufficiently housed, insufficiently clad, and insufficiently nourished, in spite

---

* We are, of course, only speaking here of the purely economic foundation of crises. Crises as results of political events (wars and serious threatenings of war) or of very widespread failures of crops—local failures no longer exercise any effect in this respect—are of course always possible.

† The use of the word " material " in the passage mentioned (Vol. II., p. 164) is not without interest in judging how Marx understood this word. According to the present usual definition of the word the explanation of crises from under-consumption would be quite as materialistic as founding it on changes in the process of production, or in implements.

of abundant means at hand for sufficient housing, nourishment, and clothing; that out of this
incongruity, over-production appears again and
again in different branches of production, so
that either actually certain articles are produced
in greater amounts than can be used—for example, more yarn than the present weaving
mills can work—or that certain articles are
produced not indeed in a greater quantity than
can be used, but in a greater quantity than can
be bought; that in consequence of this, great
irregularity occurs in the employment of the
workers, which makes their situation extremely
insecure, weighs them down in unworthy dependence, brings forth over-work here and want
of work there; and that of the means employed
to-day to counteract the most visible part of this
evil, the Kartels represent monopolist unions—
on the one side against the workers, and on the
other against the great public—which have a
tendency to carry on warfare over the heads of
these and at their cost with the same kind of
monopolist unions in other industries or other
lands, or, by international or inter-industrial
agreements, arbitrarily to adapt production and
prices to their need of profit. The capitalistic
means of defence against crises virtually bear
within themselves the possibilities of a new and
more hopeless serfdom for the working classes,
as well as of privileges of production which
revive in acute form the old guild privileges.
It appears to me to be much more important at
present, from the standpoint of the workers, to
keep before our eyes the possibilities of Kartels

and trusts than to prophesy their "impotence." It is for the working class a subordinate question whether these combinations will be able, in the course of time, to attain their first-mentioned object—the warding off of crises. But it becomes a question full of importance as soon as expectations of any kind as regards the movement for the emancipation of the working classes are made dependent upon the question of the general crisis. For then the belief that Kartels are of no effect against crises may be the cause of very disastrous neglect.

The short sketch which we gave in the introduction to this chapter of the Marx-Engels explanations of economic crises will suffice, in conjunction with the corresponding facts adduced, to show that the problem of crises cannot be solved by a few well-preserved catch-words. We can only investigate what elements of modern economy work in favour of crises and what work against them. It is impossible to pre-judge à *priori* the ultimate relation of these forces to one another, or their development. Unless unforeseen external events bring about a general crisis—and as we have said that can happen any day—there is no urgent reason for concluding that such a crisis will come to pass for purely economic reasons. Local and partial depressions are unavoidable; general stagnation is not unavoidable with the present organisation and extension of the world market, and particularly with the great extension of the production of articles of food. The latter phenomenon is of peculiar importance for

our problem. Perhaps nothing has contributed
so much to the mitigation of commercial crises
or to the stopping of their increase as the fall
of rent and of the price of food.*

---

* *Note to the English edition.*—This was written in
the winter 1898-1899 before the South African War had
produced new conditions on the money market and a
great increase in armaments. In spite of these facts the
crisis that broke out in 1901 was of shorter life than a
good many of the earlier crises, and was followed by a
longer period of prosperity.

CHAPTER III.

THE TASKS AND POSSIBILITIES OF SOCIAL DEMOCRACY.

(a) *The political and economic preliminary conditions of socialism.*

If we asked a number of men belonging to any class or party to give in a concise formula a definition of socialism, most of them would be somewhat confused. He who does not repeat at random some phrase he has heard must first make clear to himself whether he has to characterise a state, a movement, a perception, or an aim. If we consult the literature of socialism itself, we shall come across very various explanations of its concept according as they fall into one or other of the categories designated above—from the derivation of the concept from juridical notions (equality, justice) or its summary characterisation as social science, up to its identification with the class struggle of the workers in modern society and the explanation that socialism means co-operative economics. In some cases conceptions founded on entirely different principles are the grounds for this variety of explanations; but they are mostly only the results of observing or representing one and the same thing from different points of view.

The most exact characterisation of socialism will in any case be that which starts from the concept of association because by it an economical as well as—in the widest sense of the word —a juridical relation is expressed at the same time. It needs no long-winded deduction to show that the indication of the juridical nature of socialism is just as important as that of its economic nature. Quite apart from the question whether or in what sense law is a primary or secondary factor in the life of a community, the nature of its law undoubtedly in each case gives the most concentrated idea of its character. We characterise forms of communities, not according to their technological or economic foundations, but according to the fundamental principle of their legal institutions. We speak, indeed, of an age of stone, bronze, machinery, electricity, etc., but of a feudal, capitalistic, bourgeois, etc., order of society. To this would correspond the definition of socialism as a movement towards—or the state of—an order of society based on the principle of association. In this sense, which also corresponds with the etymology of the word (*socius*—a partner), the word is used in what follows.

Now what are the preliminary conditions of the realisation of socialism? Historical materialism sees them first in the modern development of production. With the spread of the capitalistic large enterprises in industry and agriculture there is assumed to be a lasting and steadily-increasing material cause for the impetus to a socialistic transformation of society. In these under-

takings production is already socially organised,
only the management is individualistic and the
profit is appropriated by individuals, not on the
ground of their labour, but of their share of
capital. The active worker is separated from
the possession of his instruments of production,
he is in the dependent condition of a wage-
earner, from which he does not escape as long
as he lives, and the pressure of it is rendered
sharper by the uncertainty which is joined with
this dependence both on the employer and on
the fluctuations in the state of trade. Like production itself, the conditions of existence for the
producers press towards the socialisation and
the co-operative organisation of production and
exchange. As soon as this development is
sufficiently advanced the realisation of socialism
becomes an imperative necessity for the further
development of the community. To carry it out
is the task of the proletariat organised as a
class party which for this purpose must take
possession of the political government.

According to that, we have as the first condition of the general realisation of socialism a
definite degree of capitalist development, and
as the second the exercise of political sovereignty by the class party of the workers, *i.e.,*
social democracy. The dictatorship of the
proletariat is, according to Marx, the form of
the exercise of this power in the transition
period.

As regards the first condition, it has already
been shown in the section on the " Classes of
Establishments in Production and Distribution"

that if the large undertaking in industry predominates to-day, yet it, including the businesses dependent on it, even in such an advanced country as Prussia, represents at the most only half the population engaged in production. The picture is not different if we take the statistics for the whole of Germany, and it is very little different in England, the most industrial country of Europe. In other foreign lands, perhaps with the exception of Belgium, the relation of the large enterprise to the small and medium business is still more unfavourable. But in agriculture we see everywhere the small and medium holding, as compared with the large one, not only greatly predominating, but also strengthening its position. In commerce and distribution the relation of the groups of undertakings is similar.

That the picture which the summarised figures of trade statistics give receives many corrections on a more recent examination of separate divisions, I have myself shown in my article on the *Catastrophic Theory,* after I had already expressly referred, in an earlier article of the series, *Problems of Socialism*, to the fact that the number of employees in an undertaking was no safe indication as to the degree of its capitalist nature.*

---

* I wrote in an earlier article of the *Problems of Socialism* concerning the subordinate and branch establishments in industry : " Such a subordinate establishment which is perhaps worked with very much constant (*i.e.*, fixed) and with very little variable (*i.e.*, wages) capital, which employs expensive machinery and few workers, comes thus, according to the practice of the

But this is of no particularly great consequence for us at present. Whether of the
hundreds of thousands of small undertakings,
a good number are of capitalistic character and
others are wholly or partly dependent on large
capitalist undertakings, this can alter very little
the total result which the statistics of undertakings offer. The great and growing variety
of undertakings, the graduated character of the
structure of industrial enterprises, is not thereby
disproved. If we strike out of the list a quarter
or even a half of all small establishments as
dependencies of medium and large enterprises,
there remain in Germany almost a million
undertakings from capitalist giant enterprises,
downward in ever broadening classes to the
hundred thousands of small enterprises worked
in handicraft fashion, which may, indeed, pay
tribute by-and-by to the process of concentration, but on that account show no indication of
disappearing from the scene.

It follows that as far as centralised enterprise
forms a preliminary condition for the socialisation of production and distribution, this is only

---

Imperial statisticians, under small factories or even small
workshops, whilst it really belongs to the capitalistic
factories. . . . We may assume it as quite certain that
handicrafts and small factories appear much stronger in
point of numbers in the trade statistics than they are in
reality " (*Neue Zeit* xv. 1, p. 308). And in respect to
agriculture : " The area can be fairly small and yet be
the scene of a thoroughly capitalistic business. Statistics
founded on the size of the establishment in area, say
less and less of their economic character " (*ibid.*, p. 380).
Similarly in my article on the *Catastrophic Theory*, on
p. 552, xvi., 1, with respect to the figures for commerce
and trade.

a partial condition in even the most advanced countries of Europe, so that if in Germany in the near future the state wished to expropriate all undertakings, say of twenty persons and upwards, be it for state management altogether or for partly managing and partly leasing them, there would still remain in commerce and industry hundreds of thousands of undertakings with over four millions of workers which would be excluded and be carried on under private management. In agriculture there would remain, if all holdings of over 20 hectares were nationalised—of which no one dreams—several millions of holdings under private management with a total of 9,000,000 workers. One can form an idea of the magnitude of the task which would be borne by the state, or the states, by taking over even the larger undertakings. It would be a question, in industry and commerce together, of about a hundred thousand businesses with five to six million employees, and in agriculture of over 300,000 holdings with over five million workers. What abundance of judgment, practical knowledge, talent for administration, must a government or a national assembly have at its disposal to be even equal to the supreme management or managing control of such a gigantic organism !

But let us leave this question on one side for a time, and let us keep first of all firmly to the fact that the material preliminary condition for the socialisation of production and distribution —advanced centralisation of enterprises—is at present only partly achieved.

The second preliminary condition, according to the theory of Marx, is the conquest of the political power by the proletariat. One can think of this conquest in various ways : by the path of parliamentary struggle, turning the right to vote to good account, or by the path of force by means of a revolution.*

It is known that Marx and Engels, until pretty recently, considered the latter as nearly everywhere absolutely inevitable, and it seems unavoidable to various adherents of the Marxist doctrine to-day. Often it is also considered the shorter way. †

---

* " Revolution " is here used exclusively in its political meaning, as synonymous with a rising or unlawful force. For the change in the order of society, on the other hand, the term " social reorganisation " is used, which leaves open the question of the way. The object of this distinction is to exclude all misunderstandings and ambiguities.

† " But to whom is it not evident that for the great towns where the workers form the overwhelming majority, if they had once attained the command of public power, of its administration, and the enactment of law—the economic revolution would have been only a question of months, nay, perhaps of weeks?" (Jules Guesde, *Der achtezehnte März* [1871] *in der Provinz. Zukunft* [1877], p. 87).

"But we declare : Give us for half a year the power of government, and the capitalist society would belong to history " (Parvus in the *Sächsiche Arbeiterzeitung*, March 6th, 1898).

The latter sentence stands at the end of an article in which, amongst other things, it is shown that even after the social revolutionary government has taken the regulation of the total production in hand, the setting up of trade in commodities by an artificially thought-out system of exchange will not be practicable. In other words, Parvus, who has occupied himself seriously with economics, understands on the one side that "the trade in commodities has permeated so deeply all conditions of social life that it cannot be replaced by an artificially

To this, people are led before all else by the idea that the working class is the most numerous and also the most energetic class of the community. Once in possession of power, it would not rest until it had substituted for the foundations of the present system such arrangements as would make its restoration impossible.

It has already been mentioned that Marx and Engels, in the establishment of their theory of the dictatorship of the proletariat, had before their eyes as a typical example the epoch of terror of the French Revolution. Even in *Anti-Dühring* Engels declares that St. Simon, in 1792, by regarding the reign of terror as the reign of the masses without means, made a discovery worthy of a genius. That is probably an over-estimation, but however highly one may esteem the discovery, the result of the rule of the men without property does not thrive much better with St. Simon than with Schiller, decried to-day as "a philistine." The men without property in 1793 were only capable of fighting the battles of others. They could only "govern" as long as the terror lasted. When

---

thought-out system of exchange," and in spite of this conviction, which has long been mine (it was already hinted at in the article on the *Sozial politische Bedeutung von Raum und Zahl*, but was to have been treated more thoroughly in a later article of the series, *Problems of Socialism*), he imagines that a social revolutionary government could in the present structure of industry "regulate" the whole of production and in half a year exterminate root and branch the capitalistic system that has grown up out of the production of commodities with which it is so intimately bound up. One sees what sort of political children the force frenzy can make out of otherwise well-informed people.

it had exhausted itself, as it was bound to do, their government was quite at an end. According to the Marx-Engels point of view, this danger would not exist with the modern proletariat. But what is the modern proletariat?

If one counts in it all persons without property, all those who have no income from property or from a privileged position, then they certainly form the absolute majority of the population of advanced countries. But this " proletariat " would be a mixture of extraordinarily different elements, of classes which have more differences among themselves than had the " people " of 1789, who certainly as long as the present conditions of property are maintained have more common—or, at least, similar—interests than contrary ones; but the different nature of their needs and interests would quickly become known to them as soon as the propertied and governing classes are removed from, or deprived of, their position.

On an earlier occasion I made the remark that the modern wage-earners are not of the homogeneous mass, devoid in an equal degree of property, family, etc., as the *Communist Manifesto* foresees; that it is just in the most advanced of the manufacturing industries that a whole hierarchy of differentiated workmen are to be found between whose groups only a moderate feeling of solidarity exists. In this remark, a well-known socialist writer, H. Cunow, sees a confirmation of the fact that even when I was speaking generally I had in my mind specially English conditions. In Germany and the other continental civilised lands he says no such separation from the revolutionary movement of the workmen in better positions is to be found as in England. In contrast to England the best-paid workmen stand at the head of the class war. The English caste feeling, he adds, is not a consequence of the social differentiation of to-day but an after-effect of the earlier system of guilds and companies and the older trade union movement based on them.

Again I must reply that what my opponent tells me is in no way new to me. If a certain guild-like feature is to be found in the English working-class movement, it is far less a heritage from the old guild system, which, indeed, existed much longer in Germany than in England, than one of the chief products of Anglo-Saxon freedom—of the fact that the English workman never, not even at the time of the suppression of the right of association, stood under the scourge of a state ruled by police. The sense of individuality is developed in freedom, or, to speak for once with Stirner, the sense of *own*. It does not exclude the recognition of what is of a different nature and of general interest, but it easily becomes the cause of a little angularity which even appears as hard and narrow-minded when it is only one-sided in form. I do not want to wrong the German workmen, and I know how fully to honour the idealism which, for example, moved the Hamburg workmen for decades to sacrifices for the common cause of the proletarian struggle for freedom which have not their equal in the working-class movement; but so far as I have opportunity of knowing and following the German working-class movement, the reactions of the trade differentiation described have asserted themselves. Special circumstances, such as the preponderance of the political movement, the long artificial suppression of trade unions, and the fact that on the whole the differences in rates of wages and hours of labour are generally less in Germany than in England, prevent their manifesting themselves in a peculiarly striking manner. But any one who follows attentively the organs of the German trade union movement will come across enough facts to confirm what I have said.

The trade unions do not create that phenomenon, they only bring it into prominence as an unavoidable result of actual differences. It cannot be otherwise than that vital differences in manner of work and amount of income finally produce different conduct and demands of life. The highly-skilled fine instrument-maker and the collier, the skilled house decorator and the porter, the sculptor or modeller and the stoker, lead, as a rule, a very different kind of life and have very different kinds of wants. Where the struggles for their standards of life lead to no collision between them, the fact that they are all wage-earners may efface these differences from their ideas, and the consciousness that they are carrying on the same kind of struggle against capital may produce a lively, mutual sympathy. Such sympathy is not wanting in England; the most aristocratic of aristocratic trade unionists have often enough shown it to workmen in worse conditions, as many of them are very good democrats in politics, if they are not socialists.* But there is a great difference between such political or social political sympathy and economic solidarity which a stronger political and economic pressure may neutralise, but which, according as this pressure diminishes, will make itself finally noticeable in one way or another. It is a great mistake to assume that England makes an exception here on principle. The same phenomenon is shown in France in another form. Similarly in Switzerland, the United States, and, as I have said, to a certain degree in Germany also.

But even if we assume that this differentiation does not exist in the industrial working classes or that it exercises no effect on the mode of thinking of the workmen concerned, yet the industrial workers are everywhere the minority of the population. In Germany, together with industrial home-workers, some 7,000,000 out of 19,000,000 people earning incomes are industrial wage-earners. We have besides the technical civil service, the shop employees, the agricultural labourers.

Here the differentiation is everywhere more marked, of which no clearer evidence is given than the painful history of the movements towards the organisation of these classes of

---

* In the socialistic movement in England, just as elsewhere, the better-paid—that is, the educated—workmen of higher mental endowment form the picked troops. One finds in the assemblies of socialist societies only very few so-called unskilled workmen.

labour in industrial unions like trade unions.*
It is quite impossible to say that the five or six
millions employed in agriculture (which the
German trade statistics register after deducting
the higher staff of assistants, stewards, etc.)
will strive to better themselves with the same
force as the industrial workers.

Only with quite a small number can one
propose or expect serious inclination for, and
understanding of, endeavours which go beyond
the mere amelioration of conditions of labour.
To by far the greatest number of them the
socialisation of agricultural production cannot
be much more than empty words. Their ideal
is in the meantime to get their own land.

Meanwhile, the desire of the industrial working classes for socialistic production is for the
most part more a matter of assumption than of
certainty. From the growth of the number
of socialist votes in public elections one can
certainly deduce a steady increase of adherents
of socialistic strivings, but no one would

---

* In the ten years since this was written a very
remarkable change for the better has taken place. The
organisations of technological, commercial, etc., functionaries and assistants have made wonderful headway.
At the end of 1907 there were, apart from the trade
unions of the wage-earners, embracing altogether
24,000,000 members, 680,981 functionaries of all sorts
and positions organised in forty-eight societies with trade
union leanings more or less distinct. Of these fifteen
societies, with altogether 459,787 members, were unions
of office, shop, warehouse, etc., functionaries and assistants in commercial and kindred enterprises. On the
other hand, there were only a few thousand agricultural
labourers organised, and not the tenth part of the organised clerks and shop assistants belonged to unions with
socialist tendencies.

maintain that all votes given to socialists come
from socialists. Even if we assumed that all
these voters would greet with joy a revolution
which brought the socialists to the helm, little
would even then be done towards the solution
of the main problem.

I think I can take it as being generally
admitted that there would be no question of an
immediate taking over by the state of the total
manufacture and distribution of products. The
state could not even take over the whole amount
of medium and large enterprises. The local
authorities, too, as connecting links, could not
do so very much. They could socialise at most
those businesses which produce, or which perform services, locally for that locality, and they
would get therewith quite a nice little task. But
can one imagine that undertakings which until
then had worked for the great outside market
could be suddenly municipalised?

Let us take an industrial town of only medium
size, say Augsburg, Barmen, Dortmund, Hanau,
Mannheim. Is anyone so foolish as to imagine
that the communes there could, in a political
crisis or at some other occasion, take over all
the different manufacturing and commercial
businesses of these places into their own
management and carry them on with success?
They would either have to leave them in the
hands of the former proprietors, or, if they
wanted to expropriate these absolutely, they
would be obliged to give them over to associations of workmen on some leasing conditions.

The question in all these cases would resolve

itself into the question of the economic power of associations—*i.e.*, of co-operation.

(b) *The Economic Capacities of Co-operative Associations.*

The question of the capabilities of associations has hitherto been treated very curiously in the Marxist literature.   If one leaves out of the question the literature of the 'sixties, one will find in it, with the exception of very general, mostly negative, observations, very little about the co-operative movement.   The reasons for this negligence are not far to seek.

First, the Marxist practice is predominantly political, and is directed towards the conquest of political power and attributes, and gives importance almost solely to the trade union movement, as a direct form of the class struggle of the workers.   But with respect to the co-operative societies, the conviction was forced on Marx that on a small scale it was fruitless, and would, moreover, have at the most only a very limited experimental value.   Only through the community could something be begun. Marx expresses himself in this sense on the associations of workmen in the *18 Brumaire.**

Later he somewhat modifies his judgment of co-operative societies to which the resolutions on the system of co-operation moved by the

---

* " It (the proletariat) partly throws itself into doctrinaire experiments, Exchange Banks, and Workmen's Associations, thus into a movement wherein it renounces the overthrowing of the old world with its own great massed-up resources."

General Council of the International at the Congress at Geneva and Lausanne bear witness, as well as the passage apparently originating from Marx, at all events approved by him in G. Eccarius' *A Workman's Refutation of John Stuart Mill*, where the same significance is applied to the associations as forerunners of the future, as the guilds had held in Rome and the early middle ages, and, further, the passage already alluded to in the third volume of *Capital*, which, written at the same time as those resolutions and Eccarius' work, brings into prominence the importance of industrial associations of the workers as a transition form to socialist production. But the letter on the draft scheme of the Gotha programme (1875) again sounds much more sceptical as regards these associations, and this scepticism reigns from the middle of the 'seventies over the whole Marxist literature.

This may partly be the result of the reaction which set in after the Paris Commune, and which gave the whole working-class movement another character almost exclusively directed towards politics. But it is also the result of the sad experiences which had been undergone everywhere with co-operative societies. The high-flown expectations to which the advance of the English co-operative movement had given occasion were not fulfilled. For all socialists of the 'sixties, societies for production had been the chief consideration, the co-operative stores were minor. The opinion prevailed—to which even Engels in his essays on the housing question gave expression—that as soon as co-operative stores everywhere included the mass of the workers they would certainly have as a consequence a reduction of wages.* The resolution drawn up by Marx for the Geneva Congress runs :—

" We recommend workmen to embark on co-operative production rather than on co-operative stores. The latter touch only the surface of the economic system of to-day, the first strikes at its foundations. . . . To stop the co-operative societies from degenerating into ordinary bourgeois companies all workers employed by them, whether shareholders or not, should receive the same share. As a merely temporary expedient it may be agreed that the shareholders should besides receive a moderate interest. "

But it was just the productive societies formed in the 'sixties which failed nearly everywhere. They had either been obliged to dissolve altogether or had dwindled into small company businesses, which, if they did not employ men for wages quite in the same way as other businesses, were weakly dying away. On the other side the societies of consumers were, or appeared to be, really turned into mere "philistine " retail shops. No wonder that people in socialist circles turned their backs more and more on the whole co-operative movement.

Two circumstances are answerable for the

---

* *Housing Question*, new edition, pp. 34-35.

fact that a comprehensive criticism on co-operation is wanting in Marx. First, at the time he wrote sufficient experience of the different forms of co-operation was wanting to formulate a judgment on that basis. The exchange bazaars which belonged to an earlier period had proved absolute failures. But, secondly, Marx did not meet the co-operative societies with that freedom from preconception which would have allowed his faculty for keen observation to penetrate further than the average socialist's. Here the already formed doctrine—or, if I may be allowed the expression, the formula—of expropriation stood in the way of his great power of analysis. The co-operative society was acceptable to him in that form in which it represented the most direct contrast to the capitalist undertaking. Hence the recommendation to workmen to take up co-operative societies for production because these attacked the existing economic system "at its foundation." That is quite in the spirit of dialectics and corresponds formally throughout with the theory of society which starts from production as, in the last instance, the decisive factor of the form of society. It corresponds also, apparently, with the conception which perceives in the antagonism between already socialised labour and private appropriation the fundamental contradiction in the modern mode of production which is pressing for a solution. Productive co-operation appears as the practical solution of this antagonism. In this sense Marx thinks of it—that is, that kind of society

where the " workers as an association are their
own capitalist,"* so that, if it necessarily
reproduced all the faults of the present system,
yet it did away in fact with the antagonism
between capital and labour and thus proved the
superfluousness of the capitalist employer. Yet
experience has since taught that industrial
co-operation constituted in just that kind of
way was not, and is not, in a position to produce
this proof; that it is the most unfortunate form
of associated labour; and that Proudhon was
actually in the right when, in regard to it, he
maintained against Louis Blanc that the
associations were " no economic force."†

The social democratic critic has sought
hitherto the causes of the economic failure of
the purely productive co-operative societies
simply in their want of capital, credit, and sale,
and has explained the decay of the associations
that have not failed economically by the corrupting influence of the capitalistic or individualistic
world surrounding them. All that is to the
point as far as it goes. But it does not exhaust
the question. Of quite a series of productive
associations that have failed financially, it is
quite certain that they had sufficient capital for

---

* Vol. III., p. 427.

† If Proudhon appears sometimes as a decided opponent
and sometimes as a supporter of co-operation, this contradiction is explained by his having at one time quite
a different form of co-operation in his mind than at
another. He refuses to the essentially monopolist association what he admits to the mutualistic association,
that is to the association working a system of reciprocity.
His criticism is, however, more intuitive than scientific,
and full of exaggerations.

their work and no greater difficulties in selling
than the average manufacturer.   If the productive association of the kind depicted had been
a force superior to the capitalistic undertaking
or even of the same economic power, then it
should at least have continued and risen in the
same ratio as the many private enterprises
begun with most modest means, and it would
not have succumbed so pitiably to the " moral "
influence of the capitalist world surrounding it,
as it has done continually again and again.
The history of the productive co-operative
societies that have not failed financially speaks
almost more loudly still against this form of
" republican factory " than that of the bankrupt
ones.   For it says that, regarding the first, the
further development means exclusiveness and
privilege.   Far from attacking the foundation
of the present economic system they have much
more given a proof of its relative strength.

On the other hand, the co-operative stores on
which the socialists of the 'sixties looked so
disparagingly, in the course of time have really
proved to be an economic power—*i.e.*, as an
organism fit to perform its work and capable of
a high degree of development.   Against the
pitiable figures which the statistics of the purely
productive co-operative societies offer, the
figures of workmen's co-operative stores show
up like the budget of a world-embracing empire
to that of a little country town.   And the workshops erected and conducted on account of such
co-operative stores have already produced many
times the amount of goods which have been

made by purely, or nearly purely, productive co-operative societies.*

The deeper reasons for the economic as well as the moral failures of purely productive associations have been excellently presented by Mrs. Beatrice Webb† in her work on the British Co-operative Movement, even if here and there, perhaps, a few exaggerations are found. For Mrs. Webb, as for the great majority of English co-operators, the society belonging to the workmen engaged in it is not socialistic or democratic but "individualistic." One can take offence at the selection of this word, but the line of thought is quite correct. This association is not socialistic, as Robertus, indeed, has already shown. When the workmen employed are the exclusive proprietors, its constitution is a living contradiction in itself. It supposes equality in the workshop, a complete democracy, a republic.

---

* The figures for the latter kind of productive co-operative societies are extremely difficult to ascertain as the official statistics of production by associations do not distinguish between them and the much more numerous and large workmen's share associations (companies) for objects of production. According to the returns of the British Board of Trade in 1897 and 1905, the value of the year's production of those associations for which the Board issued returns was :—

	1897.	1905.
Of Co-operative Stores in their own workshops	£6,100,730	£12,525,104
Of Associations of Millers' trades	1,264,402	1,128,328
Of Irish Dairy Farming Associations	353,247 ⎫	
Of Workmen's Associations for objects of Production	1,625,940 ⎬	3,683,699

Against this the registered British Co-operative Societies had in the years—

	1897.	1905.	1906.
Members	1,468,955	2,177,834	2,334,641
Capital	£24,087,430	£33,741,295	£39,898,220
Sales	56,632,450	89,403,546	98,403,692
Profit	6,402,428	10,026,387	. . . .

† Published under her maiden name, "Potter."

But as soon as it has attained a certain size—which may be relatively very modest—equality breaks down because differentiation of functions is necessary, and with it subordination. If equality is given up, the corner-stone of the building is removed, and the other stones follow in the course of time, and decay and conversion into ordinary business concerns step in. But if equality is maintained, then the possibility of extension is cut off and it remains of the small kind. That is the alternative for all purely productive associations. In this conflict they have all broken down or languished. Far from being a suitable form for removing the capitalist from the field of modern large industries they are much more a return to pre-capitalist production. That is so very much the case that the few instances where they have had relative success occurred in artisan trades, the majority of them not in England, where the spirit of large industries dominates the workers, but in strongly "small bourgeois" France. Psychologists of nations like to set England up as the land where the people seek equality in freedom, France as the land where they seek freedom in equality. The history of the French productive associations includes, indeed, many pages where the greatest sacrifices were undergone with touching devotion for the maintenance of formal equality. But it shows not one purely productive association of the modern large industry type, although the latter is nevertheless fairly widely spread in France.

Dr. Franz Oppenheimer, in his book, *Die*

*Siedlungsgenossenschaft,** has earned the merit
of materially extending and making more
thorough the investigation of Mrs. Webb. He
offers in the first chapters, in a very clearly
arranged classification, an analysis of the different forms of association which in certain parts
can scarcely be exceeded in critical clearness.
Oppenheimer brings into the classification of
associations the separation in principle between
associations for purchase and sale, the importance of which, in our opinion, he somewhat
over-estimates on single points, but which, on
the whole, must be noted as very useful and
on the basis of which a truly scientific explanation is possible of the financial and moral failure
of the purely productive associations—an explanation in which personal faults, want of
means, etc., for the first time move into the
second place, as accidental factors, which
explain the exception but not the rule. Only
to the extent to which the association is substantially an association of purchasers do its
general aims and its peculiar interests make its
extension desirable. But the more the association is one for sellers, and the more it is one
for the sale of products manufactured by itself
(the matter is somewhat modified in the case
of peasant associations), the greater is the
internal opposition. Its difficulties grow with
its growth. The risk becomes greater, the
struggle for sales more difficult; the same is
true regarding the procuring of credit, and the

---

* *Colonising Co-operative Societies.* Leipzig : Duncker
and Humblot.

fight for the profit rate or the dividends of the individual members in the general mass of profit, becomes more severe. It is therefore forced again into exclusiveness. Its interest in profit is opposed not only to that of the buyers, but also to that of all the other sellers. The association of purchasers, on the other hand, gains with growth; its interest as regards profit, if opposed to that of the sellers, is in agreement with that of all the other buyers; it strives after the keeping down of the profit rate, after cheapening of products—a pursuit of all purchasers as such, as well as of the community as a whole.

Out of this difference in the economic nature of the two kinds arises the difference in their management so clearly laid down by Mrs. Webb : the essentially democratic character of all genuine associations of purchasers, and the tendency towards an oligarchy in the character of all associations purely for sale.

The differentiation of the associations into those of purchasers and those of sellers is of value to the theory of the nature of associations because it is, in turn, connected with socialistic theory. He who objects to the terms " purchase " and " sale " as formed too specially for capitalistic production of commodities and substitutes for them the conceptions " provision " and " exchange," will then recognise all the more clearly what a much greater importance the former has for the community than has the latter. The provision of goods is the fundamental general interest. With respect to it all the members are associates in principle. All consume but all do not produce. Even the best productive association, as long as it is only an association for sale and exchange, will always stand in latent opposition to the community, will have separate interests as opposed to it. With a productive association which carries on any branch of production or public service on its own account, the community would have the same points of difference as with a capitalist undertaking, and it depends altogether on circumstances whether the arrangement with it is an easier one.

But to return to the starting-point which has led us to this discussion in the domain of the theory of associations, sufficient has been shown to prove that it is quite a mistake to believe that the modern factory produces in itself a considerable disposition for associated work. And likewise the republic in the workshop becomes a more difficult problem as the undertaking becomes greater and more complicated. For exceptional objects it may answer for men themselves to name their immediate leaders and to have the right to remove them. But for the tasks which the management of a great factory brings with it, where day by day and hour by hour prosaic decisions are to be taken which always give an opportunity for friction, it is simply impossible that the manager should be the employee of those he manages, that he should be dependent for his position on their favour and their bad temper. It has always proved impossible to continue this, and in all cases it has led to a change in the forms of the associated factory. The desire of the workers to take in hand new undertakings where they are employed as an associated manufactory and are bearing corresponding responsibilities and risks, stands in an inverse ratio to the size of their undertaking. But the difficulties grow at an increasing rate.

Let any one only for once look at the thing in the concrete and examine any large industrial undertaking, a great establishment for building machines, large electricity works, a great chemical factory, or a modern publishing business. All these and similar large industrial undertakings can certainly be quite well carried on by co-operative associations, to which also all the employees may belong, but they are absolutely unfit for the associated management of the employees themselves. It would then be shown, in the clearest way possible, what Cunow contends—viz., that the feeling of solidarity between groups of workers, different as to degree of education, manner of life, etc., is only very moderate in amount. What one usually understands by associated labour is only a mistaken rendering of the very simple forms of co-operative work as they are practised by groups, gangs, etc., of undifferentiated workers, and which, at the bottom, is only piece-work by groups.*

---

* " The thing was not easy. People like the cotton workers do not easily range themselves in the ranks of equality which are demanded for the successful conduct of a society " (*Sketch of the History of the Burnley Self-help Association* in *Co-operative Workshops in Great Britain*, p. 20).

What the community itself cannot take in hand, whether by the state, the district, or the municipality, it would do very well, especially in stormy times, to leave alone for the time being. The apparently more radical action would very soon prove to be the most in-expedient. Co-operative associations capable of living do not allow themselves to be produced by magic or to be set up by order; they must grow up. But they grow up where the soil is prepared for them.

The British co-operative societies are in possession to-day of the £15,000,000* which Lassalle considered sufficient as state credit for carrying out his association scheme. In proportion to the British national wealth that is only a small fraction; after one subtracts the capital invested abroad and the twice-reckoned capital, it is not the hundredth part of the national capital. But it does not exhaust by a great deal the British workman's capital power, and it is also steadily growing. It has nearly doubled itself in the ten years from 1887 to 1897, and has grown faster than the number of members. These rose from 851,211 to 1,468,955, the capital from 11.5 million pounds sterling to 20.4. The *production* of the societies has increased latterly still more quickly. Its value in 1894 ran only into £4,950,000 alto-gether, and in 1897 it was already almost double the amount, namely, £9,350,000.†

---

* See p. 115.

† [In 1906 the membership was 2,334,641; the capital, £39,898,000; the value of production, £13,953,828.]

These are such astonishing figures that when one reads them one asks oneself involuntarily : where are the limits of this growth? Enthusiasts on the system of co-operation have reckoned that if the British societies accumulated their profits instead of distributing them, in the course of about twenty years they would be in a position to buy the whole land of the country with all the houses and factories. That is, of course, a calculation after the manner of the wonderful calculation of compound interest on the celebrated penny invested in the year one. It forgets that there is such a thing as ground rent and assumes an increase of growth which is a physical impossibility. It overlooks the fact that it is almost impossible to win over the poorest classes to a co-operative society or that they can be won over to it only very gradually at best. It overlooks the fact that in the agricultural districts only a very limited sphere is open to a co-operative society and that it can lessen but cannot annihilate the expenses of the retail trade, so that possibilities will always spring up for the private undertakers to fit themselves into the changed conditions, and thus a retardation of its growth from a certain point of time becomes nearly a mathematical necessity. It forgets above all things, or leaves out of consideration, that without a distribution of dividends the co-operative movement would generally be at a standstill, that for large classes of the population it is just the dividend, that cursed apple of sin of the idealists of the co-operative system, which forms the chief attraction of a co-operative society. If what is often maintained to-day is very much exaggerated, namely, that the dividend of a co-operative society is no measure of the greater cheapness of its goods, that the single business sells most goods just as cheaply, on the average, as the co-operative store so that the dividend only represents the sum of small, unnoticed rises in the price of certain articles, still, the exaggeration is not altogether unfounded. The workmen's co-operative store is just as much a kind of savings bank as a means of fighting the exploitation which the parasitic retail trade means for the working classes.

But as with many persons the impulse to save is by no means very deep seated, they follow the convenience of buying at the nearest shop rather than put themselves to some trouble for the sake of the dividend. Moreover, it would be quite a mistake to say that England was originally a particularly favourable soil for co-operative societies. Quite the contrary. The habits of the working classes, the great extension in area of the towns which the cottage system brings with it, counterbalance in this respect the influence of better wages. What has been attained in England is the fruit of the hard, unflinching work of organisation.

And it is labour which was, and is, worth the trouble. Even if the co-operative store did nothing more than lower the profit rate in the retail trades, it would accomplish a work extremely useful for the national economy. And there can be no doubt that it does work in this direction. Here is a handle by means of which the working class can seize for itself a considerable portion of the social wealth which would otherwise serve to increase the income of the propertied classes and thereby strengthen them, and this, without direct destruction of life, without recourse to force which, as we have seen, is no simple affair.

We can consider it as proved that the co-operative society has shown itself to be an economic factor of importance, and if other countries are behind England in this, it has taken firm root in Germany, France, Belgium, etc., and gains ground more and more. I forebear quoting numbers because the fact is well known, and continual figures are wearisome. Of course legal trickery can hinder the spread of co-operative societies and the full development of their innate possibilities, and their success is again dependent on a certain degree of economic development; but here, we are above all concerned with showing what co-operation can do. And if it is neither necessary nor possible that the associations as we know them to-day can ever take possession of all production and distribution of commodities, and if the widening domain of public service in the state and the municipal and district councils puts limits on the other side, yet on the whole a very wide field is open to co-operation, so that, without lapsing into the co-operative Utopias I have referred to, we are justified in expecting very much from it. If in a little over fifty years out of the movement

which began with the £28 of the weavers of
Rochdale an organisation has developed which
handles a capital of £20,000,000, it would need
great courage to be willing to prophesy how
near we are to the point of time when the limit
of its growth is reached, and what forms of the
movement are still slumbering in the unknown
years of the future.

To many socialists the co-operative movement is not quite acceptable because it is too
"bourgeois." There are salaried officials and
workmen employed for wages; profits are made,
interest is paid, and disputes occur about the
amount of the dividends. Certainly if one kept
to forms, the public elementary school, for
example, is a much more socialistic institution
than the co-operative society. But the development of public services has its limits and needs
time, and meanwhile the co-operative society
is the easiest accessible form of association for
the working class, just because it is so
"bourgeois." As it is Utopian to imagine that
the community could jump into an organisation
and manner of living diametrically opposed to
those of the present day, so it would also be
Utopian to make a beginning with the most
difficult form of associated organisation.

Meanwhile co-operative production also will
be realised though probably in other forms than
the first theorists of the co-operative system
imagined. For the present moment it is the
most difficult form of the realisation of the
co-operative idea. It has already been mentioned
that the English co-operators handle more than

the £15,000,000 which Lassalle demanded for his scheme of association. And if the matter were only a financial question other pecuniary resources would be at their disposal. The friendly societies, the trade unions hardly know where to invest their accumulated funds. But it is not exactly, or not only, a question of financial resources. Nor is it a question of erecting new factories for a market already supplied. Opportunity is not lacking for buying existing and well provided factories. It is now to a great extent a question of organisation and management, and therein much is still lacking.

" Is it, in the first place, capital that we need," we read in an article in the *Co-operative News,* the central periodical of the British Society ; and the writer of the article answers the question with a decided negative. " As it appears, we have at present at our disposal some £10,000,000, which are only waiting to be employed in a co-operative way, and a further £10,000,000 could doubtless be quickly procured if we were fully in a position to apply it usefully in our movement. Do not let us, therefore, conceal the fact—for it is a fact— that even at the present hour in the co-operative world there is a greater need of more intelligence and capacity than of more money. How many among us would buy nothing that was not made and finished under co-operative conditions, if it were possible to live up to this ideal ? How many of us have not again and again attempted to use goods made by co-operators without being perfectly satisfied ?*

* December 3rd, 1898.

In other words, financial means alone will not solve the problem of co-operative work. It needs, leaving other hypotheses out of the question, its own organisation and its own leaders, and neither are improvised. Both must be sought for and tried, and it is, therefore, more than doubtful whether a point of time in which all feelings are heated and all passions excited, as in a revolution, can be in any way conducive to the solution of this problem which has already proved to be so difficult in ordinary times. In human judgment the contrary must be the case.

I have not here to enlarge on other forms of the co-operative system (loan societies, credit societies, raw materials, and warehouse associations, dairy farm associations, etc.), for these are of no importance to the wage-earning class. Nevertheless owing to the importance which the question of small farmers (who also belong to the working classes even if they are not wage earners) has for social democracy, and in view of the fact that handicrafts and small trades play a still noticeable part, at least according to the number of persons employed in them, I must point out the advance which the co-operative system has attained in these directions. The advantages of the co-operative purchase of seeds, of the co-operative purchase of machines, and the co-operative sale of produce, as well as the possibility of cheap credit, cannot save peasants already ruined, but they are a means of protecting from ruin thousands and tens of thousands of small peasants. There can be no doubt of that. There are unusually abundant opportunities to-day for the acquisition of small holdings. It would be rash to say, as some writers do, that for agriculture, with reference to the advantages of large and small undertakings, exactly the opposite law holds good as for industry. But it is not too much to say that the difference is quite extraordinary, and that the advantages which the large farm, powerful in capital and well equipped, has over the small are not so important that the small holding could not make up for them to a great extent by a fuller use of the system of cooperation. The use of mechanical power, the procuring of credit, the better security of sale— co-operation can make all these accessible to the peasant whilst the nature of his farming makes it easier for him to overcome occasional losses than is possible for the larger farmer. For the great masses of peasants are not always simply producers of commodities ; they themselves raise a considerable share of their necessary food.*

In all countries of advanced civilisation the co-operative system quickly increases in extent and scope. Belgium, Denmark, France, Holland, and lately also Ireland, show herein no different picture from Germany. It is important that social democracy instead of fishing out of statistics proofs for the preconceived theory of

---

* In Prussia, from 1895 to 1907, the small holdings of 3 to 20 hectares (7½ to 50 acres) have increased from 698,357 to 760,315, and the area they cover has also considerably increased, whilst that of the larger holdings has decreased.

the ruin of the class of small farmers should examine searchingly this question of the co-operative movement in the country and its importance. The statistics of forced sales, mortgage incumbrances, etc., are in many respects misleading. Undoubtedly landed property to-day is more mobile than ever; but this mobility does not work only from one side. Until now the openings which the forced sales have made have always been filled again.

As far as the agricultural classes are concerned we are face to face with the fact that however many co-operative arrangements they have made, one thing in co-operation has always hitherto been withheld from them: the cultivation of the land itself, that is the farming of field and meadow and actual cattle rearing. Different kinds of work linked with farming and attached to it are carried on co-operatively, or at least for co-operative societies, but farming itself withdraws here and elsewhere from co-operative work. Is co-operation less advantageous for it than for other industries? Or is it simply the peasant's landed property that stands in the way?

The fact has already been emphasised often that the division of the land among many owners is a great hindrance to the co-operative cultivation of the soil. But it does not form the only hindrance, or, to express it differently, it increases its real difficulties but is not usually the cause of them. The separation by distance of the workers, as well as the individualist character of a great part of agricultural work, plays likewise a part. It is possible that the peasants' syndicates which are still so young may get over these hindrances in their further development, or—which seems to me most probable—they will be driven gradually beyond their present limits. Meanwhile they cannot yet be reckoned with.

Even agricultural production *for* co-operative societies is at the present time an unsolved problem. The English co-operative stores have done no worse business with any undertakings than with their farms. Nowhere do the peasants gain greater profit from the soil than in Scotland. The figures of profit for wheat, oats, etc., per acre are much higher in Scotland than in England. But a farm of Scottish co-operators furnished with good machines representing a capital of £12,500 has proved a great failure. For 1894 it made a profit of six-tenths per cent., for 1895 a loss of 8.1 per cent. But how does it stand with the associations of agricultural labourers? Does the productive co-operation of agricultural labourers offer better prospects than the productive co-operation of industrial workers?

The question is all the more difficult to answer because sufficient practical examples are wanting. The classical example of such a co-operative society, the celebrated association of Ralahine, lasted too short a time (1831—1833), and whilst it lasted was too much under the influence of its founder Vandeleur and his agent Craig for it to be able to serve as a valid proof of the living power of independent

associations of workers on the land. It only
shows the great advantages of association under
certain circumstances and assumptions.

The experiences of the communistic colonies
are the same. These latter succeed in actual
or practical isolation for a long time under
circumstances one would consider most unfavourable. But as soon as they attained a
greater degree of prosperity and entered into
more intimate intercourse with the outer world
they decayed quickly. Only a strong religious
or other bond, a sectarian wall raised between
them and the surrounding world, apparently,
will keep these colonies together when they
have attained wealth. But the fact that it is
necessary for men to be limited in their development in some way, in order that such colonies
should flourish, proves that they can never be
the general type of associated labour. They
stand for Socialism at a stage of pure industrial
productive association. But they have acted as
a glowing proof of the advantages of co-
operation.

On the basis of all these facts and of the
experiments which intelligent landlords have
made with co-operative leases, sharing profits
with agricultural labourers, etc., Dr. F.
Oppenheimer has developed in the already
mentioned volume the idea of an agricultural
association which he calls " Siedlungsgenossenschaft " (Colonising Co-operative Association). It is to be an association of agricultural
labourers, or, is to begin as such, and is to
combine individual with co-operative manage-

ment—that is, small farming with associated work on a large scale, as is the case to-day on large estates where plots on the outskirts are let off in allotments at a more or less high rent, and which are often managed in a more exemplary manner. Oppenheimer conceived of a corresponding division in his Siedlungsgenossenschaft Association, only, that here the intention naturally is not to lower the price of labour for the central farming round which those small holdings are grouped, but really that opportunity shall be given to every single member to enjoy on a sufficiently large piece of land all the material and other charms of a farm of his own and to employ in its culture all the labour power not needed for the central farm of the association, which promises him the best returns or otherwise best suits his individuality. But for the rest the association is to utilise all the advantages of the modern large enterprise and all co-operative and mutual arrangements are to be adopted for the business needs, etc., of the members.

This is not the place to examine more closely the Oppenheimer proposal and the theory on which it is based. But I think I must just observe that they do not seem to me to deserve the contempt which has been their portion in some of the social democratic publications. One can doubt whether the thing can or will be worked out quite exactly in the form developed by Oppenheimer. But the fundamental thoughts which he develops depend greatly on the scientific analysis of the forms of management and agree moreover with all the experiences of co-operative practice, so that one can indeed say that if the co-operative method of farming is ever brought to pass, it can scarcely happen in any form materially different from the one worked out by Oppenheimer.*

The expropriation on a larger scale which is mostly thought of in the criticism of such proposals cannot in any case produce organic creations in a night by magic, and therefore the most powerful revolutionary government would be compelled to face the task of looking for a practical theory of co-operative work in agriculture. For such a work Oppenheimer has brought together most abundant materials and has submitted them to a sharp systematic analysis, which by itself made the " Siedlungsgenossenschaft " worth studying.

There is still one more remark to make with regard to agricultural co-operation. As far as the Socialist is a party politician he can only greet with satisfaction the present immigration from the country into the towns. It concentrates the masses of workers, revolutionises

---

* In the congress of the British Co-operative Society (Peterborough, May, 1898) a delegate, Mr. J. C. Gray, of Manchester, read a report on co-operation and agriculture, in which he, after an objective examination of all experiments made in England, finally makes a proposal which is wonderfully like Oppenheimer's project. " The soil is to be common property, the providing of all stock is to be co-operative and so is the sale of all products. But in the cultivation of the soil the individual interests must be attended to with due regard against interference with the interests of the community."—(*Co-operation and Agriculture,* Manchester, 1898, p. 9.)

their minds, and at any rate furthers emancipation. But as a theorist who thinks beyond the present day the Socialist must also say that this migration in the course of time may become too much of a good thing. It is well known to be infinitely easier to draw country people into the towns than to draw dwellers in towns into the country and accustom them to agricultural work. Thus the stream of immigration into the towns and industrial centres does not only increase the problems of the present rulers. Let us take, for example, the case of a victory of the working class democracy which brings the Socialist Party to the helm. According to all experience hitherto its immediate result would presumably be first of all to increase markedly the stream into the great towns, and it is in some measure doubtful whether the " industrial armies for agriculture " would allow themselves to be sent more willingly into the country than in France in 1848. But apart from that, the creation of co-operative associations capable of life and guidance will be under all circumstances a heavy task the further the depopulation of the country has advanced. The advantage of the existence of models of such associations would not be bought so very dearly at the price of a somewhat slower rising of the monstrous towns.*

---

* I see with pleasure that Karl Kautsky in his work on the agricultural question which has just appeared, has taken the problem of co-operation on the land seriously into examination. What he says of the obstacles that hinder the conversion of the peasants' small holdings into large associations for carrying on

(c) *Democracy and Socialism.*

" On February 24th, 1848, broke the first
dawn of a new period of history."

" Who speaks of universal suffrage utters
a cry of reconciliation."

LASSALLE, *Workers' Programme.*

The trade unions concern themselves with the
profit rate in production as the co-operative
stores concern themselves with the profit rate
on the sale of goods. The fight of the workmen
organised in trade unions for the improvement

---

agricultural work, fully agrees with what Oppenheimer
works out on the same subject. Kautsky expects the
solution of the problem from the influence of industrial developments and the conquest of political power
by the proletariat. He says evolution brings the
peasants to-day always more and more into dependence
on capitalistic enterprises, as distilleries, breweries,
sugar factories, flour mills, butter and cheese factories,
wine cellarages, etc., and makes them casual or temporary workers in other kinds of capitalist undertakings,
such as brickfields, mines, etc., where to-day small
cultivators take temporary work in order to make up for
the deficit of their holdings. With the socialisation of
all these undertakings the peasants would become " co-
operative workers," temporary workers of socialistic
associated undertakings, whilst on the other side the
proletarian revolution would lead to the conversion of
large agricultural holdings, on which to-day a great
number of the small cultivators are dependent, into
co-operative undertakings. Thus the small agricultural
holdings would lose their consistency more and more,
and their combination into co-operative holdings would
meet with fewer difficulties. Nationalisation of mort-
gages and cessation of militarism would facilitate this
evolution.

In all this there is much that is right, only Kautsky
appears to me to fall into the error of considerably over-
estimating the forces working in the direction desired
by him. Some of the industrial undertakings which he
enumerates are not on the high way to control industrially

of their standard of life is from the standpoint of the capitalist a fight between wage rate and profit rate. It is certainly too great an exaggeration to say that the changes in the rates of wages and the hours of labour have no influence at all on prices. If the wages of workers in a certain industry rise, the value of the corresponding products rises in a corresponding ratio as against the value of the product of all industries which experience no such rise in wages, and if the class of employers concerned do not succeed in meeting this rise by an improvement

---

small farms, but to become dependencies of agricultural associations and with others, as, for example, the brewing business, their connection with agricultural holdings is too loose for a change in their nature to exercise a strong reaction on the forms of the latter. It is just the largest sugar factories that belong, in Germany, to associations of big and small cultivators. Further, Kautsky allows himself, in my opinion, to be led away too much by the strong words which he now and then uses, to conclusions which would be correct if those words were true generally; but as they are only partially true, they cannot claim general acceptance. To make this clearer: In Kautsky the life of small farmers appears a sort of a hell. That can be said with justice of a great number of small farmers, but of another large number it is gross exaggeration, just as to-day in many cases one is not now justified in speaking of small farmers as "modern barbarians." It is a similar exaggeration to call the work which the small farmer performs on neighbouring estates, because his holding does not occupy him fully, slaves' work. By the use of such expressions assumptions are maintained which allow feelings and tendencies to be assumed to be general in those classes when, in reality, they are only exceptional.

If I cannot agree with all Kautsky's conclusions on the probable development of small farming, I am all the more at one with him in the principles of his agrarian political programme to be carried out by social democracy.

of machinery, they must either raise the price of the product concerned or suffer a loss in the profit rate. In this respect the different industries are very differently placed. There are industries which, on account of the nature of their products or of their monopolistic organisation, are fairly independent of the world market, and then a rise in wages is mostly accompanied by a rise in prices also, so that the profit rate does not need to fall but can even rise.*

In industries for the world market, as in all other industries where commodities produced under various conditions compete with one another, and only the cheapest command the market, the rise in wages almost always results in a lowering of profit rate. The same result occurs when, by the resistance of organised workers, an attempt fails to neutralise by a proportional lowering of wages, the lowering of prices rendered necessary by the struggle to sell. After all, a fight of the workers for wages can, in fact, be but a fight against the rise in the profit-rate at the cost of the wage-rate, however little the fighters are conscious of it at the moment.

There is no need to prove here that the fight regarding hours of labour is similarly a fight over the profit-rate. If the shorter day of labour does not directly cause a diminution in the amount of work done for the wage given

---

* Amongst others Carey relies on this partial truth in his *Doctrine of Harmony*. Certain extractive industries —mines, etc.—afford examples of it.

hitherto—in many cases it is known the reverse happens—yet it leads by a side way to an increase in the workers' demands for better conditions of life, and so makes a rise in wages necessary.

A rise in wages leading to an increase in prices does not, under certain circumstances, need to be an injury to the whole community; but is, however, more often harmful than useful in its effect. To the community, for instance, it makes no particular difference whether an industry exacts monopolist prices exclusively for a handful of employers, or whether the workers of that industry receive a certain share in such booty squeezed out of the public in general. The monopoly price is just as much worth fighting against as the cheapness of products which can only be achieved by the lowering of wages below the average minimum rate. But a rise in wages which only touches profit-rate must, under the conditions of the present day, be advantageous for the community in general. I say in general expressly, because there are also cases when the contrary is the case.

Fortunately, such extreme cases are very rare. Usually the workers know quite well how far they can go in their demands. The profit-rate, indeed, will bear a fairly strong pressure. Before the capitalist gives up his undertaking he will rather try every possible means to get a greater output for wages in other ways. The actual great differences of profit-rates in different spheres of production show that the general average profit-rate is constructed more easily in theory than even approximately realised. Instances are also not rare where even new capital that enters the market needing to be utilised does not seek the spot to which the highest profit-rate points, but, like a man in choosing his calling, allows itself to be guided by considerations in which the amount of profit takes a secondary place. Thus, even this most mighty factor for levelling profit-rates works irregularly. But the capital already invested, which greatly preponderates in each case, cannot for purely material reasons follow the movement of the profit-rate from one field of production to another. In short, the result of a rise in the price of human labour is, in by far the largest majority of cases, partly the greater perfection of machinery and the better organisation of industry, partly the more equable division of the surplus product. Both are advantageous to the general well-being. With certain limitations one can for capitalist countries modify Destutt de Tracy's well-known saying to : " Low profit-rates indicate a high degree of well-being among the mass of the people."

The trade unions are the democratic element in industry. Their tendency is to destroy the absolutism of capital, and to procure for the worker a direct influence in the management of an industry. It is only natural that great differences of opinion should exist on the degree of influence to be desired. To a certain mode of thought it may appear a breach of principle to claim less for the union than an unconditional right of decision in the trade. The knowledge that such a right under present circumstances is just as Utopian as it would be contrary to the nature of a socialist community, has led others to deny trade unions any lasting part in economic life, and to recognise them only temporarily as the lesser of various unavoidable evils. There are socialists in whose eyes the union is only an object lesson to prove the uselessness of any other than political revolutionary action. As a matter of fact, the union to-day—and in the near future —has very important social tasks to fulfil for the trades, which, however, do not demand, nor are even consistent with, its omnipotence in any way.

The merit of having first grasped the fact that trade unions are indispensable organs of the democracy, and not only passing coalitions, belongs to a group of English writers. This is not wonderful if one considers that trade unions attained importance in England earlier than anywhere else, and that England in the last third of the nineteenth century passed through a change from an oligarchic to an almost democratic state of government. The latest and most thorough work on this subject, the book on the theory and the practice of the British Trade Unions, by Sydney and Beatrice Webb, has been rightly described by the authors as a treatment of *Industrial Democracy*. Before them the late Thorold Rogers, in his lectures on the *Economic Interpretation*

of History (which, in the passing, has little in
common with the materialist conception of
history, but only touches it in single points),
called the trade union, Labour Partnership—
which comes to the same thing in principle,
but at the same time points out the limits to
which the function of a trade union can extend
in a democracy, and beyond which it has no
place in a democratic community. Independently of whether the state, the community, or
capitalists are employers, the trade union as an
organisation of all persons occupied in certain
trades can only further simultaneously the
interests of its members and the general good
as long as it is content to remain a partner.
Beyond that it would run into danger of
degenerating into a close corporation with all
the worst qualities of a monopoly. It is the
same as with the co-operative society. The
trade union, as mistress of a whole branch of
production, the ideal of various older socialists,
would really be only a monopolist productive
association, and as soon as it relied on its
monopoly or worked upon it, it would be
antagonistic to socialism and democracy, let
its inner constitution be what it may. Why
it is contrary to socialism needs no further
explanation. Associations against the community are as little socialism as is the oligarchic
government of the state. But why should such
a trade union not be in keeping with the
principles of a democracy?

This question necessitates another. What
is the principle of democracy?

The answer to this appears very simple. At first one would think it settled by the definition "government by the people." But even a little consideration tells us that by that only quite a superficial, purely formal definition is given, whilst nearly all who use the word democracy to-day understand by it more than a mere form of government. We shall come much nearer to the definition if we express ourselves negatively, and define democracy as an absence of class government, as the indication of a social condition where a political privilege belongs to no one class as opposed to the whole community. By that the explanation is already given as to why a monopolist corporation is in principle anti-democratic. This negative definition has, besides, the advantage that it gives less room than the phrase "government by the people" to the idea of the oppression of the individual by the majority which is absolutely repugnant to the modern mind. To-day we find the oppression of the minority by the majority " undemocratic," although it was originally held to be quite consistent with government by the people.* The

* The consistent advocates of Blanquism also always conceived of democracy as at first an oppressive force. Thus Hippolyte Castille publishes a preliminary introduction to his *History of the Second Republic* which culminates in a veritable glorification of the Reign of Terror. " The most perfect community," he says, " would be where tyranny was an affair of the whole community. That proves fundamentally that the most perfect society would be one where there is least freedom in the satanic (*i.e.*, individualistic) meaning of this word. . . . What is called political freedom is only a beautiful name to adorn the justifiable tyranny of the

idea of democracy includes, in the conception of
the present day, a notion of justice—an equality
of rights for all members of the community,
and in that principle the rule of the majority,
to which in every concrete case the rule of the
people extends, finds its limits. The more it
is adopted and governs the general consciousness, the more will democracy be equal in
meaning to the highest possible degree of freedom for all.

Democracy is in principle the suppression of

---

many. Political freedom is only the sacrifice of the
freedom of a number of individuals to the despotic God
of human societies, to social reason, to the social contract." "From this epoch (the time from October, 1793,
to April, 1794, when Girondists, Hebertists, Dantonists,
were beheaded one after the other) dates in truth
the re-incarnation of the principle of authority, of this
eternal defensive warfare of human societies. Freed
from the moderates and the ultras, secured against every
conflict of authority, the committee of public safety
acquires the form of government necessitated by the
given circumstances, the necessary force and unity to
maintain its position and to protect France from a
threatening anarchy. . . . No, it is not the government
that killed the first French Republic, but the Parlia-
mentarians, the traitors of Thermidor. The anarchist
and liberal republicans whose swarming hordes covered
France, continue in vain the old calumny. Robespierre
remains a remarkable man, not on account of his talents
and virtues, which are here incidental, but on account
of his genius for authority, on account of his strong
political instinct."
This worship of Robespierre was not to outlast the
second Empire. To the younger generation of the
Blanquist socialist revolutionaries who stepped on the
stage in the middle of the 'sixties and who were above
all anti-clerical, Robespierre was too philistine on account
of his Deism. They swore by Hebert and Anacharsis
Cloots. But for the rest they reasoned like Castille—
i.e., they carried out to extremes, like him, the just idea
of the subordination of individual interests to the general
interests of the community.

class government, though it is not yet the actual suppression of classes. They speak of the conservative character of the democracy, and to a certain degree rightly. Absolutism, or semi-absolutism, deceives its supporters as well as its opponents as to the extent of their power. Therefore in countries where it obtains, or where its traditions still exist, we have flitting plans, exaggerated language, zigzag politics, fear of revolution, hope in oppression. In a democracy the parties, and the classes standing behind them, soon learn to know the limits of their power, and to undertake each time only as much as they can reasonably hope to carry through under the existing circumstances. Even if they make their demands rather higher than they seriously mean in order to give way in the unavoidable compromise—and democracy is the high school of compromise—they must still be moderate. The right to vote in a democracy makes its members virtually partners in the community, and this virtual partnership must in the end lead to real partnership. With a working class undeveloped in numbers and culture the general right to vote may long appear as the right to choose " the butcher "; with the growing number and knowledge of the workers it is changed, however, into the implement by which to transform the representatives of the people from masters into real servants of the people.

Universal suffrage in Germany could serve Bismarck temporarily as a tool, but finally it compelled Bismarck to serve it as a tool. It could be of use for a time to the squires of the East Elbe district, but it has long been the terror of these same squires. In 1878 it could bring Bismarck into a position to forge the weapon of socialistic law, but through it this weapon became blunt and broken, until by the help of it Bismarck was thoroughly beaten. Had Bismarck in 1878, with his then majority, created a politically exceptional law, instead of a police one, a law which would have placed the worker outside the franchise, he would for a time have hit social democracy more sharply than with the former. It is true, he would then have hit other people also. Universal franchise is, from two sides, the alternative to a violent revolution. But universal suffrage is only a part of democracy, although a part which in time must draw the other parts after it as the magnet attracts to itself the scattered portions of iron. It certainly proceeds more slowly than many would wish, but in spite of that it is at work. And social democracy cannot further this work better than by taking its stand unreservedly on the theory of democracy·—on the ground of universal suffrage with all the consequences resulting therefrom to its tactics.

In practice—that is, in its actions—it has in Germany always done so. But in their explanations its literary advocates have often acted otherwise, and still often do so to-day. Phrases which were composed in a time when the political privilege of property ruled all over Europe, and which under these circumstances were explanatory, and to a certain degree also justified, but which to-day are only a dead weight, are treated with such reverence as though the progress of the movement depended on them and not on the understanding of what can be done, and what should be done. Is there any sense, for example, in maintaining the phrase of the " dictatorship of the proletariat " at a time when in all possible places representatives of social democracy have placed themselves practically in the arena of Parliamentary work, have declared for the proportional representation of the people, and for direct legislation—all of which is inconsistent with a dictatorship.

The phrase is to-day so antiquated that it is only to be reconciled with reality by stripping the word dictatorship of its actual meaning and attaching to it some kind of weakened interpretation. The whole practical activity of social democracy is directed towards creating circumstances and conditions which shall render possible and secure a transition (free from convulsive outbursts) of the modern social order into a higher one. From the consciousness of being the pioneers of a higher civilisation, its adherents are ever creating fresh inspiration and zeal. In this rests also, finally, the moral justification of the socialist expropriation towards which they aspire. But the " dictatorship of the classes " belongs to a lower civilisation, and apart from the question of the expediency and practicability of the thing, it is only to be looked upon as a reversion, as

political atavism. If the thought is aroused
that the transition from a capitalist to a socialist
society must necessarily be accomplished by
means of the development of forms of an age
which did not know at all, or only in quite an
imperfect form, the present methods of the
initiating and carrying of laws, and which was
without the organs fit for the purpose, reaction
will set in.

I say expressly transition from a capitalist
to a socialist society, and not from a " civic
society," as is so frequently the expression used
to-day. This application of the word " civic "
is also much more an atavism, or in any case
an ambiguous way of speaking, which must be
considered an inconvenience in the phraseology
of German social democracy, and which forms
an excellent bridge for mistakes with friend
and foe. The fault lies partly in the German
language, which has no special word for the
idea of the citizen with equal civic rights
separate from the idea of privileged citizens.

What is the struggle against, or the abolition of, a civic society? What does it mean
specially in Germany, in whose greatest and
leading state, Prussia, we are still constantly
concerned with first getting rid of a great part
of feudalism which stands in the path of civic
development? No man thinks of destroying
civic society as a civilised ordered system of
society. On the contrary, social democracy
does not wish to break up this society and make
all its members proletarians together; it
labours rather incessantly at raising the worker

from the social position of a proletarian to that of a citizen, and thus to make citizenship universal. It does not want to set up a proletarian society instead of a civic society, but a socialist order of society instead of a capitalist one. It would be well if one, instead of availing himself of the former ambiguous expression, kept to the latter quite clear declaration. Then one would be quite free of a good portion of other contradictions which opponents, not quite without reason, assert do exist between the phraseology and the practice of social democracy. A few socialist newspapers find a pleasure to-day in forced anti-civic language, which at the most would be in place if we lived in a sectarian fashion as anchorites, but which is absurd in an age which declares it to be no offence to the socialist sentiment to order one's private life throughout in a "bourgeois fashion."*

Finally, it is to be recommended that some moderation should be kept in the declaration of war against "liberalism." It is true that the great liberal movement of modern times arose

---

* In this point Lassalle was much more logical than we are to-day, granted that it was one-sidedness to derive the idea of the bourgeois simply from political privilege instead of at least from his economic position of power also. But for the rest he was sufficient realist to blunt beforehand the point of the above contradiction when he declared in the *Workers' Programme* : "In the German language the word ' bourgeoisie ' had to be translated by ' Bürgerthum ' (citizendom). But it has not this meaning with me. We are *all* citizens (' Bürger ')—the workman, the poor citizen, the rich citizen, and so forth. In the course of history the word ' bourgeoisie ' has rather acquired a meaning by which

for the advantage of the capitalist bourgeoisie
first of all, and the parties which assumed the
names of liberals were, or became in due
course, simple guardians of capitalism.
Naturally, only opposition can reign between
these parties and social democracy. But with
respect to liberalism as a great historical
movement, socialism is its legitimate heir, not
only in chronological sequence, but also in its
spiritual qualities, as is shown moreover in
every question of principle in which social
democracy has had to take up an attitude.

Wherever an economic advance of the
socialist programme had to be carried out in
a manner, or under circumstances, that
appeared seriously to imperil the development
of freedom, social democracy has never shunned
taking up a position against it. The security
of civil freedom has always seemed to it to
stand higher than the fulfilment of some
economic progress.

The aim of all socialist measures, even of
those which appear outwardly as coercive
measures, is the development and the securing
of a free personality. Their more exact

---

to denote a well defined, political line of thought "
(*Collected Works*, II., p. 27). What Lassalle further
says there of the distorted logic of Sansculottism is
especially to be recommended to writers in the *belles
lettres* style who study the middle class "naturalistically"
in the *café* and then judge the whole class according to
their dried fruits, as the philistine thinks he sees the
type of the modern workman in his fellow tippler. I
feel no hesitation in declaring that I consider the middle,
class—not excepting the German—in their bulk to be
still fairly healthy, not only economically, but also
morally.

examination always shows that the coercion included will raise the sum total of liberty in society, and will give more freedom over a more extended area than it takes away. The legal day of a maximum number of hours' work, for example, is actually a fixing of a minimum of freedom, a prohibition to sell freedom longer than for a certain number of hours daily, and, in principle, therefore, stands on the same ground as the prohibition agreed to by all liberals against selling oneself into personal slavery. It is thus no accident that the first country where a maximum hours' day was carried out was Switzerland, the most democratically progressive country in Europe, and democracy is only the political form of liberalism. Being in its origin a counter-movement to the oppression of nations under institutions imposed from without or having a justification only in tradition, liberalism first sought its realisation as the principle of the sovereignty of the age and of the people, both of which principles formed the everlasting discussion of the philosophers of the rights of the state in the seventeenth and eighteenth centuries, until Rousseau set them up in his *Contrat Social* as the fundamental conditions of the legitimacy of every constitution, and the French Revolution proclaimed them—in the Democratic Constitution of 1793 permeated with Rousseau's spirit*—as inalienable rights of men.

---

* Sovereignty "rests with the people. It is indivisible, imprescriptible, inalienable " (Article 25). " A people has at any time the right to revise, reform and alter its constitution. No generation can bind the next to its laws " (Article 28).

The Constitution of 1793 was the logical expression of the liberal ideas of the epoch, and a cursory glance over its contents shows how little it was, or is, an obstacle to socialism. Baboeuf, and the believers in absolute equality, saw in it an excellent starting point for the realisation of their communistic strivings, and accordingly wrote "The Restoration of the Constitution of 1793" at the head of their demands.

There is actually no really liberal thought which does not also belong to the elements of the ideas of socialism. Even the principle of economic personal responsibility which belongs apparently so entirely to the Manchester School cannot, in my judgment, be denied in theory by socialism nor be made inoperative under any conceivable circumstances. Without responsibility there is no freedom; we may think as we like theoretically about man's freedom of action, we must practically start from it as the foundation of the moral law, for only under this condition is social morality possible. And similarly, in our states which reckon with millions, a healthy social life is, in the age of traffic, impossible if the economic personal responsibility of all those capable of work is not assumed. The recognition of individual responsibility is the return of the individual to society for services rendered or offered him by society.

Perhaps I may be allowed to quote some passages from my article on *The Social-Political Meaning of Space and Numbers.*

" Changes in the economic personal responsibility of those capable of work can, then, as far as we can see, only be made relatively. Labour statistics can be developed very much more, the exchange or adjustment of labour be very much perfected, the change of work be made easier and a right of the workers developed which renders possible an infinitely greater security of existence and facility for the choice of a calling than are given to-day. The most advanced organs of economic self-help—the great trade unions—already point out in this respect the way which evolution will presumably take. . . . If already strong trade unions secure to those of their members fit to work a certain right of occupation, when they impress the employers that it is very inadvisable to dismiss a member of the union without very valid reasons recognised also by the union, if they in giving information to members seeking occupation supply their wants in order of application, there is in all this an indication of the development of a democratic right to work."* Other beginnings of it are found to-day in the form of industrial courts, trades councils, and similar creations in which democratic self-government has taken shape, though still often imperfectly. On the other side, doubtless, the extension of the public services, particularly of the system of education and of reciprocal arrangements (insurances, etc.) helps very much towards divesting economic personal responsibility of

* *Neue Zeit* xv. 2, p. 141.

its hardness. But a right to work, in the sense that the state guarantees to everyone occupation in his calling, is quite improbable in a visible time, and also not even desirable. What its pleaders want can only be attained with advantage to the community in the way described by the combination of various organs, and likewise the common duty to work can only be realised in this way without a deadening bureaucracy. In such great and complicated organisms as our modern civilised states and their industrial centres an absolute right to work would simply result in disorganisation; it is " only conceivable as a source of the most odious arbitrariness and everlasting quarrelling."*

Liberalism had historically the task of breaking the chains which the fettered economy and the corresponding organisations of law of the middle ages had imposed on the further development of society. That it at first strictly maintained the form of bourgeois liberalism did not stop it from actually expressing a very much wider-reaching general principle of society whose completion will be socialism.

Socialism will create no new bondage of any kind whatever. The individual is to be free, not in the metaphysical sense, as the anarchists dreamed—*i.e.*, free from all duties towards the community—but free from every economic compulsion in his action and choice of a calling. Such freedom is only possible for all by means of organisation. In this sense one might call

---

* Ibid.

socialism "organising liberalism," for when one examines more closely the organisations that socialism wants and how it wants them, he will find that what distinguishes them above all from the feudalistic organisations, outwardly like them, is just their liberalism, their democratic constitution, their accessibility. Therefore the trade union, striving after an arrangement similar to a guild, is, in the eyes of the socialist, the product of self-defence against the tendency of capitalism to overstock the labour market; but, at the same time, just on account of its tendency towards a guild, and to the degree in which that obtains, is it an unsocialistic corporate body.

The work here indicated is no very simple problem; it rather conceals within itself a whole series of dangers. Political equality alone has never hitherto sufficed to secure the healthy development of communities whose centre of gravity was in the giant towns. It is, as France and the United States show, no unfailing remedy against the rank growth of all kinds of social parasitism and corruption. If solidity did not reach so far down in the constitution of the French nation, and if the country were not so well favoured geographically, France would have long since been ruined by the land plague of the official class which has gained a footing there. In any case this plague forms one of the causes why, in spite of the great keenness of the French mind, the industrial development of France remains more backward than that of the neighbouring

countries. If democracy is not to excel centralised absolutism in the breeding of bureau-
cracies, it must be built up on an elaborately
organised self-government with a corresponding
economic, personal responsibility of all the
units of administration as well as of the adult
citizens of the state. Nothing is more injurious
to its healthy development than enforced uniformity and a too abundant amount of pro-
tectionism or subventionism.

To create the organisations described—or,
so far as they are already begun, to develop
them further—is the indispensable preliminary
to what we call socialism of production.
Without them the so-called social appropriation
of the means of production would only result
presumably in reckless devastation of productive forces, insane experimentalising and aim-
less violence, and the political sovereignty of
the working class would, in fact, only be carried
out in the form of a dictatorial, revolutionary,
central power, supported by the terrorist
dictatorship of revolutionary clubs. As such it
hovered before the Blanquists, and as such it
is still represented in the *Communist Manifesto*
and in the publications for which its authors
were responsible at that time. But "in presence
of the practical experiences of the February
revolution and much more of those of the Paris
Commune when the proletariat retained political power for two months," the revolutionary
programme given in the *Manifesto* has " here
and there become out of date." " The Commune notably offers a proof that the working

class cannot simply take possession of the state machinery and set it in motion for their own ends.''

So wrote Marx and Engels in 1872 in the preface to the new edition of the *Manifesto*. And they refer to the work, *The Civil War in France*, where this is developed more fully. But if we open the work in question and read the part referred to (it is the third), we find a programme developed which, according to its political contents, shows in all material features the greatest similarity to the federalism of Proudhon.

'' The unity of the nation was not to be broken, but on the contrary it was to be organised by the destruction of that power of the state which pretended to be the personification of that unity but wanted to be independent of, and superior to, the nation on whose body it was after all only a parasitic growth. Whilst they were occupied in cutting off the merely oppressive organs of the old governing power its rightful functions as a power which claimed to stand above the community were to be taken away and given over to the responsible servants of the community. Instead of deciding once in three or six years what member of the ruling class should trample on and crush the people in Parliament, universal suffrage should serve the people constituted in communities, as individual suffrage serves every other employer to select for his business workers, inspectors, and clerks.''

'' The antagonism between the commune and

the power of the state has been looked on as an exaggerated form of the old fight against over-centralisation. . . . The constitution of the commune, on the contrary, would have restored to the community all the powers which until now the parasitic growth, the state, which lives on the community and hinders its free action, has absorbed.''

Thus Marx wrote in the *Civil War in France*.

Let us now listen to Proudhon. As I have not his work on Federalism at hand, a few sentences may follow here from his essay on the *Political Capacity of the Working Classes*, in which he incidentally preaches the forming of the workers into a party of their own.

'' In a democracy organised according to the true ideas of the sovereignty of the people, *i.e.,* according to the fundamental principles of the right of representation, every oppressive and corrupting action of the central authority on the nation is rendered impossible. The mere supposition of such a thing is absurd.''

'' And why?

'' Because in a truly free democracy the central authority is not separated from the assembly of delegates, the natural organs of local interests called together for agreement. Because every deputy is, first of all, the man of the locality which named him its representative, its emissary, one of its fellow-citizens, its special agent to defend its special interests, or to bring them as much as possible into union with the interests of the whole community before the great jury (the nation); because

the combined delegates, if they choose from
their midst a central executive committee of
management, do not separate it from themselves or make it their commander who can
carry on a conflict with them.

" There is no middle course; the commune
must be sovereign or only a branch [of the
state]—everything or nothing. Give it, however pleasant a part to play, from the moment
when it does not create its rights out of itself,
when it must recognise a higher law, when the
great group to which it belongs is declared to
be superior to it and is not the expression of
its federated relations, they will unavoidably
find themselves one day in opposition to each
other and war will break out." But then logic
and power will be on the side of the central
authority. " The idea of a limitation of the
power of the state by means of groups, when
the principle of subordination and centralisation
rules in regard to these groups themselves, is
inconsistent, not to say contradictory." It is
the municipal principle of bourgeois liberalism.
A " federated France " on the other hand, " a
régime which represents the ideal of independence and whose first act would consist in
restoring to the municipalities their full independence and to the Provinces their self-
government "—that is the municipal freedom
which the working class must write on its
flag.*   And if in the *Civil War* we find that
" the political sovereignty of the producers

* *Capacité Politique des Classes Ouvrières*, pp. 224,
225, 231, 235.

cannot exist with the perpetuation of their
social slavery," we read in the *Capacité
Politique* : "When political equality is once
given by means of universal suffrage, the
tendency of the nation will be towards economic
equality. That is just how the workmen's
candidates understood the thing. But this is
what their bourgeois rivals did not want.* In
short, with all the other differences between
Marx and the "petit bourgeois," Proudhon,
on this point, their way of thinking is as nearly
as possible the same.

There is not the least doubt (and it has since
then been proved many times practically) that
the general development of modern society is
along the line of a constant increase of the
duties of municipalities and the extension of
municipal freedom, that the municipality will
be an ever more important lever of social
emancipation. It appears to me doubtful if it
was necessary for the first work of democracy
to be such a dissolution of the modern state
system and complete transformation of its
organisation as Marx and Proudhon pictured
(the formation of the national assembly out of
delegates from provincial or district assemblies,
which in their turn were composed of delegates
from municipalities) so that the form the
national assemblies had hitherto taken had to
be abolished. Evolution has given life to too
many institutions and bodies corporate, whose
sphere has outgrown the control of municipalities and even of provinces and districts for it

* *Id.*, p. 214.

to be able to do without the control of the central governments unless or before their organisation is transformed. The absolute sovereignty of the municipality, etc., is besides no ideal for me. The parish or commune is a component part of the nation, and hence has duties towards it and rights in it. We can as little grant the district, for example, an unconditional and exclusive right to the soil as we can to the individual. Valuable royalties, rights of forest and river, etc., belong, in the last instance, not to the parishes or the districts, which indeed only are their usufructuaries, but to the nation. Hence an assembly in which the national, and not the provincial or local, interest stands in the forefront or is the first duty of the representatives, appears to be indispensable, especially in an epoch of transition. But beside it, those other assemblies and representative bodies will attain an ever greater importance, so that Revolution or not, the functions of the central assemblies become constantly narrowed, and therewith the danger of these assemblies or authorities to the democracy is also narrowed. It is already very little in advanced countries to-day.

But we are less concerned here with a criticism of separate items in the quoted programme than with bringing into prominence the energy with which it emphasises autonomy as the preliminary condition of social emancipation, and with showing how the democratic organisation from the bottom upwards is depicted as the way to the realisation of socialism, and how the antagonists Proudhon and Marx meet again in—liberalism.

The future itself will reveal how far the municipalities and other self-governing bodies will discharge their duties under a complete democracy, and how far they will make use of these duties. But so much is clear : the more suddenly they come in possession of their freedom, the more experiments they will make in number and in violence and therefore be liable to greater mistakes, and the more experience the working class democracy has had in the school of self-government, the more cautiously and practically will it proceed.

Simple as democracy appears to be at the first glance, its problems in such a complicated society as ours are in no way easy to solve. Read only in the volumes of *Industrial Democracy* by Mr. and Mrs. Webb how many experiments the English trade unions had to make and are still making in order to find out the most serviceable forms of government and administration, and of what importance this question of constitution is to trade unions. The English trade unions have been able to develop in this respect for over seventy years in perfect freedom. They began with the most elementary form of self-government and have been forced to convince themselves that this form is only suited to the most elementary organisms, for quite small, local unions. As they grew they gradually learned to renounce as injurious to their successful development certain cherished ideas of doctrinaire democracy (the imperative mandate, the unpaid official, the powerless central representation), and to form instead of it a democracy capable of governing with representative assemblies, paid officials, and central government with full powers. This section of the history of the development of "trade union democracy" is extremely instructive. If all that concerns trade unions does not quite fit the units of national administration, yet much of it does. The chapter referred to in *Industrial Democracy* belongs to the theory of democratic government. In the history of the development of trade unions is shown how the executive central management—their state government—can arise simply from division of labour which becomes necessary through the extension in area of the society and through the number of its members. It is possible that with the socialist development of society this centralisation may also later on become superfluous. But for the present it cannot be dispensed with in democracy. As was demonstrated at the end of the first division of this chapter it is an impossibility for the municipalities of great towns or industrial centres to take over under their own management all local productive and commercial undertakings. It is also, on practical grounds, improbable—not to mention grounds of equity which are against it—that they should " expropriate " those undertakings each and all offhand in a revolutionary upheaval. But even if they did (whereby in the majority of cases would only empty husks come into their hands) they would be obliged to lease

the mass of the businesses to associations,
whether individual or trade union, for associated
management.*

In every one of these cases, as also in the
municipal and national undertakings, certain
interests of the different trades would have to be
protected, and so there would always remain
a need for active supervision on the part of
trade unions. In the transition period particularly, the multiplicity of organs will be of great
value.

Meantime we are not yet so far on, and it is
not my intention to unfold pictures of the
future. I am not concerned with what will
happen in the more distant future, but with
what can and ought to happen in the present,
for the present and the nearest future. And so
the conclusion of this exposition is the very banal
statement that the conquest of the democracy,
the formation of political and social organs of
the democracy, is the indispensable preliminary
condition to the realisation of socialism.

Feudalism, with its unbending organisations
and corporations, had to be destroyed nearly
everywhere by violence. The liberal organisations of modern society are distinguished from
those exactly because they are flexible, and
capable of change and development. They do
not need to be destroyed, but only to be further
developed. For that we need organisation and

---

* This would certainly bring about complicated
problems. Think of the many joint undertakings of
modern times which employ members of all possible
trades.

energetic action, but not necessarily a revolutionary dictatorship. "As the object of the class war is especially to destroy distinctions of class," wrote some time since (October, 1897) a social democratic Swiss organ, the *Vorwärts* of Basle, " a period must logically be agreed upon in which the realisation of this object, of this ideal, must be begun. This beginning, these periods following on one another, are already founded in our democratic development; they come to our help, to serve gradually as a substitute for the class war, to absorb it into themselves by the building up of the social democracy." "The bourgeoisie, of whatever shade of opinion it may be," declared lately the Spanish socialist, Pablo Iglesias, " must be convinced of this, that we do not wish to take possession of the Government by the same means that were once employed, by violence and bloodshed, but by lawful means which are suited to civilisation " (*Vorwärts,* October 16th, 1898). From a similar point of view the *Labour Leader,* the leading organ of the English Independent Labour Party, agreed unreservedly with the remarks of Vollmar on the Paris Commune. But no one will accuse this paper of timidity in fighting capitalism and the capitalist parties. And another organ of the English socialist working class democracy the *Clarion,* accompanied an extract from my article on the theory of catastrophic evolution with the following commentary :

" The formation of a true democracy—I am quite convinced that that is the most pressing and most important duty which lies before us. This is the lesson which the socialist campaign of the last ten years has taught us. That is the doctrine which emerges out of all my knowledge and experiences of politics. We must build up a nation of democrats before socialism is possible."

(d) *The most pressing Problems of Social Democracy.*

"And what she is, that dares she to appear."—SCHILLER, *Maria Stuart.*

The tasks of a party are determined by a multiplicity of factors : by the position of the general, economic, political, intellectual and moral development in the sphere of its activity, by the nature of the parties that are working beside it or against it, by the character of the means standing at its command, and by a series of subjective, ideologic factors, at the head of them, the principal aim of the party and its conception of the best way to attain that aim. It is well known what great differences exist in the first respect in different lands. Even in countries of an approximately equal standard of industrial development, we find very important political differences and great differences in the conceptions and aspirations of the mass of the people. Peculiarities of geographical situation, rooted customs of national life, inherited institutions, and traditions of all kinds create a difference of mind which only slowly submits to the influence of that development. Even where socialist parties have originally taken the same hypotheses for the starting point of their work, they have found themselves obliged in the course of time to adapt their activity to the special conditions of their country. At a given moment, therefore, one can probably set up general political principles of social democracy with a claim that they apply to all countries, but no programme of action applicable for all countries is possible.

As shown above, democracy is a condition of socialism to a much greater degree than is usually assumed, *i.e.,* it is not only the means but also the substance. Without a certain amount of democratic institutions or traditions, the socialist doctrine of the present time would not indeed be possible. There would, indeed, be a workers' movement, but no social democracy. The modern socialist movement—and also its theoretic explanation—is actually the product of the influence of the great French Revolution and of the conceptions of right which through it gained general acceptance in the wages and labour movement. The movement itself would exist without them as, without and before them, a communism of the people was linked to primitive Christianity.*

---

* It has repeatedly happened to me (and certainly also to others) in former years that at the conclusion of a propagandist meeting labourers and workmen who had heard a socialist speech for the first time would come to me and declare that what I had said was already to be found in the Bible ; they could show me the passages, sentence for sentence.

But this communism of the people was very indefinite and half mythical, and the workers' movement would lack inner cohesion without the foundation of those organisations and conceptions of law which, at least to a great part, necessarily accompany capitalist evolution. A working class politically without rights, grown up in superstition and with deficient education, will certainly revolt sometimes and join in small conspiracies, but never develop a socialist movement. It requires a certain breadth of vision and a fairly well developed consciousness of rights to make a socialist out of a workman who is accidentally a revolter. Political rights and education stand indeed everywhere in a prominent position in the socialist programme of action.

So much for a general view. For it does not lie in the plan of this work to undertake an estimation of individual points of the socialist programme of action. As far as concerns the immediate demands of the Erfurt programme of the German social democracy, I do not feel in any way tempted to propose changes with respect to them. Probably, like every social democrat, I do not hold all points equally important or equally expedient. For example, it is my opinion that the administration of justice and legal assistance free of charge, under present conditions, is only to be recommended to a limited degree, that certainly arrangements should be made to make it possible for those without means to seek to have a chance of getting their rights;

but that no pressing need exists to take over the mass of the property law suits to-day and put the lawyers completely under the control of the State. Meanwhile, although legislators of to-day will hear nothing of such a step, as a socialist legislature cannot be achieved without a full reform of the legal system, or only according to such newly created legal institutions, as, for example, exist already in arbitration courts for trade disputes, the said demand may keep its place in the programme as an indication of the development striven after.

I gave a very definite expression to my doubt as to the expediency of the demand in its present form as early as in 1891, in an essay on the draft scheme of the programme then under discussion, and I declared that the paragraph in question gave "too much and too little."* The article belongs to a series which Kautsky and I then drew up jointly on the programme question, and of which the first three essays were almost exclusively the mental work of Kautsky, whilst the fourth was composed by me. Let me here quote two sentences from it which indicate the point of view which I upheld at that time with regard to the action of social democracy, and which will show how much or how little my opinions have changed since then :—

" To demand simply the maintenance of all those without employment out of the state money means to commit to the trough of the

---

* *Neue Zeit* ix. 2, § 221.

state not only everyone who cannot find work but everyone that will not find work. . . . . One need really be no anarchist in order to find the eternal heaping of duties on the state too much of a good thing. We will hold fast to the principle that the modern proletarian is indeed poor but that he is no pauper. In this distinction lies a whole world, the nature of our fight, the hope of our victory."

" We propose the formula : ' Conversion of the standing armies to citizen armies ' because it maintains the aim and yet leaves the party a free hand to-day (when the disbanding of standing armies is utterly impossible) to demand a series of measures which narrow as much as possible the antagonism between army and people as, for example, the abolition of special military courts of justice, lessening of time of service, etc."*

But has social democracy, as the party of the working classes and of peace, an interest in the maintenance of the fighting power? From many points of view it is very tempting to answer the question in the negative, especially if one starts from the sentence in the *Communist Manifesto* : " The proletarian has no fatherland." This sentence might, in a degree, perhaps, apply to the worker of the 'forties without political rights, shut out of public life. To-day in spite of the enormous increase in the intercourse between nations it has already forfeited a great part of its truth and will always forfeit more, the

---

* Pp. 819, 824, 825

more the worker, by the influence of socialism, moves from being a proletarian to a citizen. The workman who has equal rights as a voter for state and local councils, and who thereby is a fellow owner of the common property of the nation, whose children the community educates, whose health it protects, whom it secures against injury, has a fatherland without ceasing on that account to be a citizen of the world, just as the nations draw nearer one another, without, therefore, ceasing to lead a life of their own.

The complete breaking up of nations is no beautiful dream, and in any case is not to be expected in the near future. But just as little as it is to be wished that any other of the great civilised nations should lose its independence, just as little can it be a matter of indifference to German social democracy whether the German nation, which has indeed carried out, and is carrying out, its honourable share in the civilising work of the world, should be repressed in the council of the nations.

In the foregoing is shown in principle the point of view from which the social democracy has to take its position under present conditions with regard to questions of foreign politics. If the worker is still no full citizen, he is not without rights in the sense that national interests can be indifferent to him. And if also social democracy is not yet in power, it already takes a position of influence which lays certain obligations upon it. Its words fall with great weight in the scale. With the present composition of the army and the complete uncertainty as to the changes in methods of war, etc., brought about by the use of guns of small bore, the Imperial Government will think ten times before venturing on a war which has social democracy as its determined opponent. Even without the celebrated general strike social democracy can speak a very important, if not decisive, word for peace, and will do this according to the device of the International as often and as energetically as it is necessary and possible. It will also, according to its programme, in the cases when conflicts arise with other nations and direct agreement is not possible, stand up for settling the difference by means of arbitration. But it is not called upon to speak in favour of renunciation of the preservation of German interests, present or future, if or because English, French, or Russian Chauvinists take umbrage at the measures adopted. Where, on the German side, it is not a question merely of fancies or of the particular interests of separate groups which are indifferent or even detrimental to the welfare of the nation, where really important national interests are at stake, internationalism can be no reason for a weak yielding to the pretensions of foreign interested parties.

This is no new idea, but simply the putting together of the lines of thought which lie at the bottom of all the declarations of Marx, Engels, and Lassalle on the questions of foreign politics. It is also no attitude endangering peace which is here recommended. Nations to-day no longer lightly go to war, and a firm stand can under some circumstances be more serviceable to peace than continuous yielding.

The doctrine of the European balance of power seems to many to be out of date to-day, and so it is in its old form. But in a changed form the balance of power still plays a great part in the decision of vexed international questions. It still comes occasionally to the question of how strong a combination of powers supports any given measure in order that it may be carried through or hindered. I consider it a legitimate task of German Imperial politics to secure a right to have a voice in the discussion of such cases, and to oppose, on principle, proper steps to that end, I consider, falls outside the domain of the tasks of social democracy.

To choose a definite example. The leasing of the Kiauchow Bay at the time was criticised very unfavourably by the socialist press of Germany. As far as the criticism referred to the circumstances under which the leasing came about, the social democratic press had a right, nay, even a duty, to make it. Not less right was it to oppose in the most decided way the introduction of or demand for a policy of partition of China because this partition did not lie at all in the interest of Germany. But if some papers went still further and declared that the party must under all circumstances and as a matter of principle condemn the acquisition of the Bay, I cannot by any means agree with it.

It is a matter of no interest to the German people that China should be divided up and Germany be granted a piece of the Celestial Empire. But the German people has a great interest in this—that China should not be the prey of other nations; it has a great interest in this—that China's commercial policy should not be subordinated to the interest of a single foreign power or a coalition of foreign powers—in short, that in all questions concerning China, Germany should have a word to say. Its commerce with China demands such a right to protest. In so far as the acquisition of the Kiauchow Bay is a means of securing this right to protest, and it will be difficult to gainsay that it does contribute to it, there is no reason in my opinion for the social democracy to cry out against it on principle. Apart from the manner in which it was acquired and the pious words with which it was accompanied, it was not the worst stroke of Germany's foreign policy.

It was a matter of securing free trade with and in China. For there can be no doubt that without that acquisition China would have been drawn to a greater degree into the ring of the capitalist economy, and also that without it Russia would have continued its policy of encircling, and would have occupied the Manchurian harbours. It was thus only a question as to whether Germany should look on quietly whilst, by the accomplishment of one deed after another, China fell ever more and more into dependence on Russia, or whether Germany should secure herself a position on the ground that she also, under normal conditions, can make her influence felt at any time on the situation of things in China, instead of being obliged to content herself with belated protests. So far ran and runs the leasing of the Kiauchow Bay, a pledge for the safeguarding of the future interests of Germany in China, be its official explanation what it may, and thus far could social democracy approve it without in the least giving away its principles.

Meanwhile, owing to the want of responsibility in the management of the foreign policy of Germany, there can be no question of positive support from the social democracy, but only of the right foundation of its negative attitude. Without a guarantee that such undertakings should not be turned to account over the heads of the people's representative House for other aims than those announced, say as a means to achieve some temporary success which might surrender the greater interests of the future, without some such pledge social democracy can take upon itself no share in the measures of foreign policy.

As can be seen the rule here unfolded for the position regarding questions of foreign policy turns on the attitude observed hitherto in practice by social democracy. How far it agrees in its fundamental assumptions with the ruling mode of viewing things in the party, does not lie with me to explain. On the whole, tradition plays a greater part in these things than we think. It lies in the nature of all advanced parties to lay only scanty weight on changes already accomplished. The chief object they have in view is always that which does not change—quite a justifiable and useful tendency towards definite aims—the setting of goals. Penetrated by this, such parties fall easily into the habit of maintaining longer than is necessary or useful opinions handed down from the past, in assumptions of which very much has been altered. They overlook or undervalue these changes; they seek for facts which may still make those opinions seem valid, more than they examine the question whether in the face of the totality of the facts appertaining to it, the old opinion has not meanwhile become prejudice.

Such political à *priori* reasoning often appears to me to play a part in dealing with the question of colonies.

In principle it is quite a matter of indifference to-day to socialism, or the workmen's movement, whether new colonies should prove successful or not. The assumption that the extension of colonies will restrict the realisation of socialism, rests at bottom on the altogether outworn idea that the realisation of socialism depends on an increasing narrowing of the circle of the well-to-do and an increasing misery of the poor. That the first is a fable was shown in earlier chapters, and the misery theory has now been given up nearly

everywhere, if not with all its logical conclusions and outright, yet at least by explaining
it away as much as possible.*

But even if the theory were right, the

---

* H. Cunow makes such an attempt in his article
The Catastrophe. He says that if Marx at the end of
his first volume of *Capital* speaks of the "increasing
mass of misery" which will appear with the progress
of capitalist production we must understand by that "not
a simple retrogression of the social state of existence of
the worker" but only a "retrogression of his social total
position in relation to progressive, civilised development
—that is, in relation to the increase of productivity and
the increase of the general wants of civilisation." The
idea of misery is no fixed one. " What appears to one
workman in a certain category, whom a great difference
in education separates from his 'master of work,' as a
lot worthy to be striven after, may appear to a well-
qualified worker of another category, who mentally,
perhaps, is intellectually superior to his 'master of work,'
as such a ' mixture of misery and oppression ' that he
rises in revolt against it " (*Neue Zeit* xvii., pp. 402-403).

Unfortunately Marx speaks in the sentence referred to
not only of the increasing mass of misery, of oppression,
but also of " slavery, of deterioration, of exploitation."
Are we to understand these also in the implied—" Pick-
wickian"—sense? Are we to admit, perhaps, a deterioration of the worker which is only a relative deterioration
in proportion to the increase of the general civilisation?
I am not inclined to do it, nor Cunow probably. No,
Marx speaks in the passage referred to quite positively
of " a constantly decreasing number of millionaires "
who " usurp all the advantages " of the capitalist
transformation and the growth " of the man of misery,
of oppression," etc. (*Capital,* I., chap. xxiv. 7). One
can ground the catastrophe theory on this contrast, but
not on the moral misery caused by the intellectually
inferior managers who are to be found in every counting
house—in every hierarchical organisation.

Incidentally it is a little satisfaction to me to see how
Cunow here can only reconcile with reality the sentences
on which the catastrophe theory rests by suddenly allow-
ing workers of different categories to appear with
fundamentally opposed social ideas? Are those, then,
also " English workers "?

colonies about which there is now an interest
in Germany are far from being in the position
to re-act so quickly on social conditions at
home, that they could only keep off a possible
catastrophe for a year. In this respect the
German social democracy would have nothing
to fear from the colonial policy of the German
Empire. And because it is so, because the
development of the colonies which Germany
has acquired (and of those which it could perhaps win, the same holds good) will take so
much time that there can be no question for
many a long year of any reaction worth
mentioning on the social conditions of Germany. Just from this reason the German
social democracy can treat the question of
these colonies without prejudice. There can
even be no question of a serious reaction of
colonial possessions on the political conditions
of Germany. Naval Chauvinism, for
example, stands undoubtedly in close connection with colonial Chauvinism, and draws
from it a certain nourishment. But the first
would also exist without the second, just as
Germany had her navy before she thought of
the conquest of colonies. It must nevertheless
be granted that this connection is the most
rational ground for justifying a thorough
resistance to a colonial policy.

Otherwise, there is some justification during
the acquisition of colonies to examine carefully
their value and prospects, and to control the
settlement and treatment of the natives as
well as the other matters of administration;

but that does not amount to a reason for considering such acquisition beforehand as something reprehensible.

Its political position, owing to the present system of government, forbids social democracy from taking more than a critical attitude to these things, and the question whether Germany to-day needs colonies can, particularly in regard to those colonies that are still to be obtained, be answered in the negative with good authority. But the future has also its rights for us to consider. If we take into account the fact that Germany now imports yearly a considerable amount of colonial produce, we must also say to ourselves that the time may come when it will be desirable to draw at least a part of these products from our own colonies. However speedy socialists may imagine the course of development in Germany towards themselves to be, yet we cannot be blind to the fact that it will need a considerable time before a whole series of other countries are converted to socialism. But if it is not reprehensible to enjoy the produce of tropical plantations, it cannot be so to cultivate such plantations ourselves. Not the whether but the how is here the decisive point. It is neither necessary that the occupation of tropical lands by Europeans should injure the natives in their enjoyment of life, nor has it hitherto usually been the case. Moreover, only a conditional right of savages to the land occupied by them can be recognised. The higher civilisation ultimately can claim a higher right. Not the conquest, but the cultivation, of the land gives the historical legal title to its use.*

According to my judgment these are the essential points of view which should decide the position of social democracy as regards the question of colonial policy. They also, in practice, would bring about no change worth mentioning in the vote of the party; but we are not only concerned, I repeat, with what would be voted in a given case, but also with the reasons given for the vote.

There are socialists to whom every admission of national interests appears as Chauvinism or as an injury to the internationalism and class policy of the proletariat. As in his time Domela Nieuwenhuis declared Bebel's well-known assertion—that in case of an attack on the part of Russia the social democracy would set up their men for the defence of Germany—to be Chauvinism, so lately, Mr. Belfort Bax also found reprehensible jingoism in a similar assertion by Mr. Hyndman.†

---

* " Even a whole society, a nation, nay, all contemporaneous societies taken together are not proprietors of the earth. They are only its tenants, its usufructuaries, and have to leave it improved as *boni patres familias* to the following generation" (Marx, *Capital*, III. 2, p. 309).

† Hyndman insists with great decision on the idea that England, for the protection of the importation of its foodstuffs, needs a navy large enough for every possible combination of adversaries. " Our existence as a nation of free men depends on our supremacy at sea. This can be said of no other people of the present day. However much we socialists are naturally opposed to armaments, we must, however, recognise facts" (*Justice*, December 31st, 1898).

It must be admitted that it is not always
easy to fix the boundary where the advocacy of
the interests of one's nation ceases to be just and
to pass into pseudo-patriotism; but the remedy
for exaggeration on this side certainly does not
lie in greater exaggeration on the other. It
is much more to be sought in a movement for
the exchange of thought between the demo-
cracies of the civilised countries and in the
support of all factors and institutes working
for peace.

Of greater importance to-day than the
question of raising the demands already
standing on the programme, is the question
of supplementing the party's programme.
Here practical development has placed a
whole series of questions on the orders of the
day which at the drawing up of the programme
were partly considered to be lying away too far
in the future for social democracy to concern
itself specially with them, but which were also
partly, not sufficiently considered in all their
bearings. To these belong the agrarian
question, the policy of local administration,
co-operation and different matters of industrial
law. The great growth of social democracy in
the eight years since the drawing up of the
Erfurt Programme, its reaction on the home
politics of Germany as well as its experiences
in other lands, have made the more intimate
consideration of all these questions imperative,
and many views which were formerly held
about them have been materially corrected.

Concerning the agrarian question, even those

who thought peasant cultivation doomed to
decay have considerably changed their views
as to the length of time for the completion
of this decay. In the later debates on the
agrarian policy to be laid down by the social
democracy, certainly many differences of opinion
have been shown on this point, but in principle
they revolved round this—whether, and in a
given case to what limit, social democracy
should offer assistance to the peasant as an
independent farmer against capitalism.

The question is more easily asked than
answered. The fact that the great mass of
peasants, even if they are not wage earners,
yet belong to the working classes, *i.e.,* do not
maintain existence merely on a title to possessions or on a privilege of birth, places them
near the wage-earning class. On the other
side they form in Germany such an important
fraction of the population that at an election
in very many constituencies their votes decide
between the capitalist and socialist parties.
But if social democracy would not or will
not limit itself to being the party of the
workers in the sense that it is only the political
completion of trade unionism, it must be careful
to interest at least a great part of the peasants
in the victory of its candidates. In the long
run that will only happen if social democracy
commits itself to measures which offer an
improvement for the small peasants in the
immediate future. But with many measures
having this object the legislature cannot distinguish between the small and the middle class

peasants, and on the other hand they cannot help the peasant as a citizen of the state or as a worker without supporting him at least indirectly as an "undertaker."

This is shown with other things in the programme of socialist agrarian policy which Kautsky sketched at the end of his work on the agrarian question under the heading *The Neutralisation of the Peasantry*. Kautsky shows most convincingly that even after a victory for social democracy no reason will exist for the abolition of peasants' holdings. But he is at the same time a strong opponent of such measures, or the setting up of such demands, as aim at forming a "protection for peasants" in the sense that they would retain the peasant artificially as an undertaker. He proposes quite a series of reforms, or declares it admissible to support them, which result in relieving the country parishes and in increasing their sources of income. But to what class would these measures be a benefit in the first instance? According to Kautsky's own representation, to the peasants. For, as he shows in another passage of his work, in the country, even under the rule of universal suffrage, there could be no question of an influence of the proletariat on the affairs of the parish worth mentioning. For that influence is, according to him, too isolated, too backward, too dependent on the few employers of labour who control it. "A communal policy other than one in the interest of the landowner is not to be thought of." Just as little can we

think to-day " of a modern management of the
land by the parish in a large co-operative
farming enterprise controlled by the village
community."* But, so far, and so long, as
that is so, measures like " Amalgamation of
the hunting divisions of the great landowners
in the community," " Nationalisation of the
taxes for schools, roads, and the poor," would
obviously contribute to the improvement of the
economic position of the peasants and therewith
also to the strengthening of their possessions.
Practically, then, they would just work as
protection for the peasants.

Under two hypotheses the support of such
protection for the peasants appears to me
innocuous. First a strong protection of agricultural labourers must go hand in hand with
it, and secondly democracy must rule in the
commune and the district. Both are assumed
by Kautsky. But Kautsky undervalues the
influence of agricultural labourers in the
democratised country parish. The agricultural
labourers are as helpless as he describes them
in the passage quoted, only in such districts as
lie quite outside commercial intercourse; and
their number is always becoming smaller.
Usually the agricultural labourer is to-day
tolerably conscious of his interests and with
universal suffrage would even become more so.
Besides that, there exist in most parishes all
kinds of antagonisms among the peasants
themselves, and the village community contains, in craftsmen and small traders, elements

* *The Agrarian Question*, pp. 337 and 338.

which in many respects have more in common with the agricultural labourers than with the peasant aristocracy. All that means that the agricultural labourers, except in a very few cases, would not have to make a stand alone against an unbroken "reactionary mass." Democracy has, in the country districts, if it is to exist, to work in the spirit of socialism. I consider democracy in conjunction with the results of the great changes in the system of communication, of transport, a more powerful lever in the emancipation of agricultural labourers than the technical changes in peasant farming.

I refrain from going through all the details of Kautsky's programme with which, as I have already remarked, I agree thoroughly in principle; but I believe that a few observations on it ought not to be suppressed. For me, as already observed, the chief task which social democracy now has to fulfil for the agricultural population can be classified under three heads, namely : (1) *The struggle against all the present remnants and supports of feudal landowners, and the fight for democracy in the commune and district.* This involves a fight for the removal of entail, of privileged estate parishes, hunting privileges, etc., as laid down by Kautsky. In Kautsky's formulation "the fullest self-government in the parish and the province," the word "fullest" does not seem to me well chosen, and I would substitute for it the word "democratic." Superlatives are nearly always misleading. "Fullest self-government " can apply to the circle of those entitled to have a say, what it means can be better expressed by " democratic self-government "; but it can also denote the administrative functions, and then it would mean an absolutism of the parish, which neither is necessary nor can be reconciled with the demands of a healthy democracy. The general legislature of the nation stands above the parish, apportioning its definite functions and representing the general interests against its particular interests.

(2) *Protection and relief of the working classes in agriculture.* Under this heading falls the protection of labourers in the narrower sense : Abolition of regulations for servants, limitation of hours of labour in the various categories of wage earners, sanitary police regulations, a system of education, as well as measures which free the small peasant as a taxpayer.

(3) *Measures against the absolutism of property and furthering co-operation.* Hereunder would fall demands like " Limitation of the rights of private property in the soil with a view to promoting (1) the suppression of adding field to field, (2) the cultivation of land, (3) prevention of disease " (Kautsky); " reduction of exorbitant rents by courts of justice set up for the purpose " (Kautsky); the building of healthy and comfortable workmen's dwellings by the parish; "facilities for co-operative unions by means of legislation " (Kautsky); the right of the parish to acquire land by purchase or expropriation and to lease it at a

cheap rent to workmen and workmen's associations.

This latter demand leads to the question of co-operation. After what has been said in the chapter on the economic possibilities of co-operative associations I need say little here. The question to-day is no longer whether co-operative associations ought to exist or not. They exist and will exist whether the social democracy desires it or not. By the weight of its influence on the working classes, social democracy certainly can retard the spread of workmen's co-operative societies, but it will not thereby do any service for itself or the working class. The hard-and-dry Manchesterism which is often manifested by sections of the party in regard to co-operation and is grounded on the declaration that there can be no socialist co-operative society within a capitalist society is not justified. It is, on the contrary, important to take a decided position and to be clear which kind of associations social democracy can recommend, and can morally support.

We have seen what an extraordinary advance associations for credit, purchasing, dairy farming, working and selling, make in all modern countries. But these associations in Germany are generally associations of peasants, representatives of the " middle class movement " in the country. I consider it incontrovertible that they, in conjunction with the cheapening of the rate of interest which the increased accumulation of capital brings with it, could indeed help much towards keeping peasant enterprises capable of competing with large enterprises. Consequently, these peasant associations are in most cases the scene of the action of anti-socialist elements, of *petits bourgeois* liberals, clericals, and anti-semites. So far as social democracy is concerned, they can to-day be put out of reckoning nearly everywhere—even if in their ranks there are here and there small peasants who are nearer to the socialist than to other parties. The middle-class peasant takes the lead with them. If social democracy ever had a prospect of winning a stronger influence on the class of the country population referred to by means of co-operation, it has let the opportunity slip.

But if the social democratic party has not the vocation of founding co-operative stores, that does not mean it should take no interest in them. The dearly-loved declaration that co-operative stores are not socialist enterprises, rests on the same formalism which long acted against trade unions, and which now begins to make room for the opposite extreme. Whether a trade union or a workmen's co-operative store is or is not socialistic, does not depend on its form but on its character—on the spirit that permeates it. They are not socialism, but as organisations of workmen they bear in themselves enough of the element of socialism to develop into worthy and indispensable levers for the socialist emancipation. They will certainly best discharge their economic tasks if they are left completely to themselves in their organisation and government. But as the aversion and even enmity which many socialists formerly felt against the trade union movement has gradually changed into friendly neutrality and then into the feeling of belonging together, so will it happen with the stores—so has it already happened in some measure.

Those elements, which are enemies not only of the revolutionary, but of every emancipation movement of the workers, by their campaign against the workmen's co-operative stores have obliged the social democracy to step in to support them. Experience has also shown that such fears, as that the co-operative movement would take away intellectual and other forces from the political movement of the workers, were utterly unfounded. In certain places that may be the case temporarily, but in the long run exactly the opposite takes place. Social democracy can look on confidently at the founding of working men's co-operative stores where the economic and legal preliminary conditions are found, and it will do well to give it its full good-will and to help it as much as possible.

Only from one point of view could the workmen's co-operative store appear something doubtful in principle—namely, as the good which is in the way of the better, the better being the organisation of the purchase and the distribution of commodities through the municipality, as is designed in nearly all socialist systems. But first of all the democratic store, in order to embrace all members of the place

in which it is located, needs no alteration in
principle, but only a broadening of its constitution, which throughout is in unison with
its natural tendencies (in some smaller places
co-operative stores are already not far from
counting all the inhabitants of the place as
their members). Secondly, the realisation of
this thought still lies such a long way off, and
assumes so many political and economic
changes and intermediate steps in evolution,
that it would be mad to reject with regard to
it all the advantages which the workers can
draw to-day from the co-operative store. As
far as the district council or parish is concerned
we can only through it to-day provide clearly
defined, general needs.

With that we come now to the borough or
municipal policy of social democracy. This
also for a long time was the step-child of the
socialist movement. It is, for example, not
very long ago that in a foreign socialist paper
(which has since disappeared), edited by very
intellectual folk, the following idea was rejected
with scorn as belonging to the *petit bourgeois,*
namely, the using of municipalities as the lever
of the socialist work of reform without, on
that account, neglecting parliamentary action,
and the beginning through the municipality
of the realisation of socialist demands. The
irony of fate has willed it that the chief editor
of that paper was only able to get into the
Parliament of his country on a wave of municipal socialism. Similarly in England, social
democracy found in the municipalities a rich

field of fruitful activity before it succeeded in sending its own representatives to Parliament. In Germany the development was different. Here social democracy had long obtained Parliamentary civil rights before it gained a footing to any extent worth mentioning in the representative bodies of the communes. With its growing extension its success also increased in the elections for local bodies, so that the need for working out a socialist municipal programme has been shown more and more, and such has already been drawn up in individual states or provinces. What does social democracy want for the municipality, and what does it expect from the municipality?

With regard to this the Erfurt programme says only " Self-government of the people in empire, state, province, and municipality; election of officials by the people," and demands for all elections the direct right to vote for all adults. It makes no declaration as to the legal relation of the enumerated governing bodies to one another. As shown farther back, I maintain that the law or the decree of the nation has to come from the highest legal authority of the community—the state. But that does not mean that the division line between the rights and powers of the state and the municipality should always be the same as to-day.

To-day, for example, the municipal right of expropriation is very limited, so that a whole series of measures of an economic-political character would find in the opposition, or exaggerated demands, of town landlords a positively insurmountable barrier. An extension of the law of expropriation should accordingly be one of the next demands of municipal socialism. It is not, however, necessary to demand an absolutely unlimited law of expropriation. The municipality would always be bound to keep to the regulations of the common law which protect the individual against the arbitrary action of accidental majorities. Rights of property which the common law allows must be inviolable in every community so long as, and in the measure in which, the common law allows them. To take away lawful property otherwise than by compensation, is confiscation, which can only be justified in cases of extreme pressure of circumstances—war, epidemics.*

---

* I gave expression to this idea very energetically some years ago in my summary of Lassalle's *System of Acquired Rights*, which work is itself, as Lassalle writes, dedicated to the object of reconciling revolutionary law with positive law. Braving the danger of being charged with thinking as a philistine, I have no hesitation in declaring that to me the thought or proposal of an expropriation, which would only be robbery dressed up in a legal form, appears wholly objectionable—not to speak of an expropriation according to the prescription of Barères—and, quite apart from the fact that such an expropriation would be objectionable on purely economic or utilitarian grounds. "Whatever far-reaching encroachments on the domain of the privileges of property prevailing hitherto one may assume in this respect, in the period of transition to a socialist state of society, they cannot be those of a senseless operating brutal force, but they must be the expression of an idea of law, even if it be new and asserts itself with elementary force " (Complete Edition of Lassalle's *Works*, vol. iii., p. 791). The form of the expropriation of the expropriators corresponding most nearly to the socialistic conception of law and rights is that of a replacement by the activities of organisations and institutions.

Social democracy will thus be obliged to demand for the municipality, when the franchise becomes democratic, an extension of the right of expropriation (which is still very limited in various German states) if a socialist policy of local government is to be possible. Further, demands respecting the creation of municipal enterprises and of public services, and a labour policy for the municipality, are rightly put into the forefront of the programme. With respect to the first, the following demand should be set up as essential, that all enterprises having a monopolist character and being directed towards the general needs of the members of the municipality must be carried out under its own management, and that, for the rest, the municipality must strive constantly to increase the area of the service it gives to its members. As regards labour policy, we must demand from the municipalities that they, as employers of labour, whether under their own management or under contract, insert as a minimum condition the clauses for wages and hours of labour recognised by the organisations of such workmen, and that they guarantee the right of combination for these workmen. It should, however, be observed here that if it is only right to endeavour to make municipalities as employers of labour surpass private firms with regard to conditions of labour and arrangements for the welfare of the workers, it would be a shortsighted policy for municipal workmen to demand such conditions as would place them, when compared with their fellow-workers in the same trades, in the position of an unusually privileged class, and that the municipality should work at a considerably higher cost than the private employer. That would, in the end, lead to corruption and a weakening of public spirit.

Modern evolution has assigned to municipalities further duties : the establishment and superintendence of local sick funds, to which perhaps at a not very distant epoch the taking over of insurance against invalidity will be added. There has further been added the establishment of labour bureaux and industrial arbitration courts. With regard to the labour bureaux the social democracy claims as its minimum demand that their character should be guaranteed by their being composed of an equal representation of workmen and employers; that arbitration courts should be established by compulsion and their powers extended. Social democracy is sceptical of, even if it does not protest against, municipal insurance against unemployment, as the idea prevails that this insurance is one of the legitimate duties of trade unions and can best be cared for by them. But that can only hold good for well-organised trades which unfortunately still contain a small minority of the working population. The great mass of workers is still unorganised, and the question is whether municipal insurance against unemployment can, in conjunction with trade unions, be so organised that, so far from being an encroachment on the legitimate functions of the latter, it may even be a means of helping them. In any case it would be the duty of the social democratic representatives of the municipality, where such insurance is undertaken, to press with all their energy for the recognition of the unions.*

From its whole nature, municipal socialism is an indispensable lever for forming or completely realising what I, in the last chapter, called " the democratic right of labour." But it is and must be patch-work where the franchise of the municipality is class franchise. That is the case in more than three-fourths of Germany. And so we stand here, as we do with reference to the diets of the federal states, on which the municipalities depend to a great extent, and to the other organs of self-government (districts, provinces, etc.), face to face with the question : how will social democracy succeed in removing the existing class franchise and in obtaining the democratisation of the electoral systems?

Social democracy has to-day in Germany, besides the means of propaganda by speech and writing, the franchise for the Reichstag as the most effective means of asserting its demands. Its influence is so strong that it has extended even to those bodies which have been made inaccessible to the working class owing to a property qualification, or a system of class franchise; for parties must, even in these

---

* Since the above was written the question has in several German towns been solved by a municipal contribution to the unemployed funds of the unions.

assemblies, pay attention to the electors for the Reichstag. If the right to vote for the Reichstag were protected from every attack, the question of treating the franchise for other bodies as a subordinate one could be justified to a certain extent, although it would be a mistake to make light of it. But the franchise for the Reichstag is not secure at all. Governments and government parties will certainly not resolve lightly on amending it, for they will say to themselves that such a step would raise amongst the masses of the German workers a hate and bitterness, which they would show in a very uncomfortable way on suitable occasions. The socialist movement is too strong, the political self-consciousness of the German workers is too much developed, to be dealt with in a cavalier fashion. One may venture, also, to assume that a great number even of the opponents of universal suffrage have a certain moral unwillingness to take such a right from the people. But if under normal conditions the curtailing of the franchise would create a revolutionary tension, with all its dangers for the governing classes, there can, on the other hand, be no doubt as to the existence of serious technical difficulties in the way of altering the franchise so as to allow, only as an exception, the success of independent socialist candidatures. It is simply political considerations which, on this question, determine the issue.

On this and other grounds it does not seem advisable to make the policy of social democracy

solely dependent on the conditions and possibilities of the imperial franchise. We have,
moreover, seen that progress is not so quickened
by it as might have been inferred from the
electoral successes of 1890 and 1893. Whilst
the socialist vote in the triennial period from
1887 to 1890 rose 87 per cent., and from 1890
to 1893 25 per cent., in the five years from
1893 to 1898 it only rose 18 per cent.—an
important increase in itself, but not an increase
to justify extraordinary expectations in the
near future.

Now social democracy depends not exclusively on the franchise and Parliamentary
activity. A great and rich field exists for it
outside Parliaments. The socialist working
class movement would exist even if Parliaments
were closed to it. Nothing shows this better
than the gratifying movements among the
Russian working classes. But with its exclusion from representative bodies the German
working class movement would, to a great
extent, lose the cohesion which to-day links
its various sections; it would assume a chaotic
character, and instead of the steady, uninterrupted forward march with firm steps, jerky
forward motions would appear with inevitable
back-slidings and exhaustions.

Such a development is neither in the interest
of the working classes nor can it appear
desirable to those opponents of social democracy who have become convinced that the
present social order has not been created for
all eternity but is subject to the law of change,

and that a catastrophic development with all
its horrors and devastation can only be avoided
if in legislation consideration is paid to changes
in the conditions of production and commerce
and to the evolution of the classes. And the
number of those who recognise this is steadily
increasing. Their influence would be much
greater than it is to-day if the social democracy
could find the courage to emancipate itself from
a phraseology which is actually outworn and
if it would make up its mind to appear what it
is in reality to-day : a democratic, socialistic
party of reform.

It is not a question of renouncing the so-
called right of revolution, this purely speculative
right which can be put in no paragraph of a
constitution and which no statute book can
prohibit, this right which will last as long as
the law of nature forces us to die if we abandon
the right to breathe. This imprescriptible and
inalienable right is as little touched if we place
ourselves on the path of reform as the right of
self-defence is done away with when we make
laws to regulate our personal and property
disputes.

But is social democracy to-day anything
beyond a party that strives after the socialist
transformation of society by the means of
democratic and economic reform? According
to some declarations which were maintained
against me at the congress in Stuttgart this
might perhaps appear to be the case. But in
Stuttgart my letter was taken as an accusation
against the party for sailing in the direction of

Blanquism, whilst it was really directed against some persons who had attacked me with arguments and figures of speech of a Blanquist nature and who wanted to obtain from the congress a pronouncement against me.

Even a positive verdict from the Stuttgart Congress against my declaration would not have diverted me from my conviction that the great mass of the German social democracy is far removed from fits of Blanquism. After the speech at Oeynhausen I knew that no other attitude of the congress was to be expected than the one which it in fact adopted.*

The Oeynhausen speech has since then shared the fate of so many other speeches of extraordinary men, it has been semi-officially corrected. And in what sense has the party expressed itself since Stuttgart? Bebel, in his speeches on the attempts at assassination, has entered the most vigorous protests against the idea that social democracy upholds a policy of force, and all the party organs have reported these speeches with applause; no protest against them has been raised anywhere. Kautsky develops in his *Agrarian Question* the principles of the agrarian policy of social

---

* " Some days before the Stuttgart Congress on the 6th September, 1898, William II. at Oeynhausen, Westphalia, announced a law threatening with penal servitude those who dared to prevent a man from working or incited him to strike. That such a speech should create a revolutionary mood amongst German social democrats was the most natural thing in the world. But the threat came to nought. The Reichstag rejected a Bill on the subject by a large majority, although it was only a diluted edition of that announced by the Kaiser. The fate of the speech confirmed my assertions."

democracy. They form a system of thoroughly democratic reform just as the Communal Programme adopted in Brandenburg is a democratic programme of reform. In the Reichstag the party supports the extension of the powers and the compulsory establishment of courts of arbitration for trades disputes. These are organs for the furtherance of industrial peace. All the speeches of their representatives breathe reform. In the same Stuttgart where, according to Clara Zetkin, the " Bernstein-iade " received the finishing stroke, shortly after the Congress, the social democrats formed an alliance with the middle-class democracy for the municipal elections, and their example was followed in other Wurtemberg towns. In the trade union movement one union after another proceeds to establish funds for out-of-work members, which practically means a giving up of the characteristics of a purely fighting coalition, and declares for municipal labour bureaux embracing equally employers and employees; whilst in various large towns—Hamburg, Elberfeld—co-operative stores have been started by socialists and trade unionists. Everywhere there is action for reform, action for social progress, action for the victory of democracy. " People study the details of the problems of the day and seek for levers and starting points to carry on the development of society in the direction of socialism." Thus I wrote a year ago,* and I see no reason to induce me to delete a word of it.

* The Struggle of Social Democracy and the Revolution of Society.—Neue Zeit xvi., 1, p. 451.

Conclusion.

Ultimate Aim and Tendency.—Kant against Cant.

Reference has already been made in different passages of this book to the great influence which tradition exercises, even amongst socialists, upon judgments regarding facts and ideas. I say expressly " even amongst socialists " because this power of tradition is a very widespread phenomenon from which no party, no literary or artistic line of thought, is free, and which penetrates deeply even into most of the sciences. It will probably never be quite rooted out. A certain interval of time must always pass before men so far recognise the inconsistency of tradition with what exists as to put the former on the shelf. Until this happens tradition usually forms the most powerful means of linking those together whom no strong, constant, effective interest or external pressure knits together. Hence the intuitive preference of all men of action, however revolutionary they may be in their aims, for tradition. " Never swop horses whilst crossing a stream." This motto of old Lincoln is rooted in the same thought as Lassalle's well-known anathema against the " nagging spirit of liberalism, the complaint of individual opining and wanting to know better." Whilst tradition is essentially conservative, criticism is almost always destructive. At the moment of important action, therefore, criticism, even when most justified by facts, can be an evil, and therefore be reprehensible.

To recognise this is, of course, not to call tradition sacred and to forbid criticism. Parties are not always in the midst of rapids when attention is paid to one task only.

For a party which has to keep up with a real evolution, criticism is indispensable and tradition can become an oppressive burden, a restraining fetter.

But men in very few cases willingly and fully account for the importance of the changes which take place in their traditional assumptions. Usually they prefer to take into account only such changes as are concerned with undeniable facts and to bring them into unison as far as can be with the traditional catchwords. The method is called pettifogging, and the apologies and explanations for it are called cant.

Cant—the word is English, and is said to have been first used in the sixteenth century as a description of the saintly sing-song of the Puritans. In its more general meaning it denotes an unreal manner of speech, thoughtlessly imitative, or used with the consciousness of its untruth, to attain any kind of object, whether it be in religion, politics, or be concerned with theory or actuality. In this wider meaning cant is very ancient—there were no worse "canters," for example, than the Greeks of

the past classic period—and it permeates in
countless forms the whole of our civilised life.
Every nation, every class and every group
united by theory or interest has its own cant.
It has partly become such a mere matter of
convention, of pure form, that no one is any
longer deceived by its emptiness, and a fight
against it would be shooting idly at sparrows.
But this does not apply to the cant that appears
in the guise of science and the cant which has
become a political battle cry.

My proposition, " To me that which is generally called the ultimate aim of socialism is
nothing, but the movement is everything," has
often been conceived as a denial of every
definite aim of the socialist movement, and
Mr. George Plechanow has even discovered
that I have quoted this " famous sentence "
from the book *To Social Peace,* by Gerhard
von Schulze-Gävernitz. There, indeed, a
passage reads that it is certainly indispensable
for revolutionary socialism to take as its ultimate aim the nationalisation of all the means
of production, but not for practical political
socialism which places near aims in front of
distant ones. Because an ultimate aim is here
regarded as being dispensable for practical
objects, and as I also have professed but little
interest for ultimate aims, I am an " indis-
criminating follower " of Schulze-Gävernitz.
One must confess that such demonstration bears
witness to a striking wealth of thought.

When eight years ago I reviewed the Schulze-
Gävernitz book in *Neue Zeit,* although my

criticism was strongly influenced by assumptions which I now no longer hold, yet I put on
one side as immaterial that opposition of ultimate aim and practical activity in reform, and
admitted—without encountering a protest—
that for England a further peaceful development,
such as Schulze-Gävernitz places in prospect
before her was not improbable. I expressed
the conviction that with the continuance of free
development, the English working classes
would certainly increase their demands, but
would desire nothing that could not be shown
each time to be necessary and attainable beyond all doubt.   That is at the bottom nothing
else than what I say to-day.   And if anyone
wishes to bring up against me the advances in
social democracy made since then in England,
I answer that with this extension a development of the English social democracy has gone
hand in hand from the Utopian, revolutionary
sect, as Engels repeatedly represented it to be,
to the party of political reform which we now
know.*   No socialist capable of thinking,
dreams to-day in England of an imminent
victory for socialism by means of a violent
revolution—none dreams of a quick conquest of
Parliament by a revolutionary proletariat.   But
they rely more and more on work in the municipalities and other self-governing bodies.   The
early contempt for the trade union movement
has been given up; a closer sympathy has been

* I use the words " social democracy " here in the
wider sense of the whole independent socialist movement. (English edition.)

won for it and, here and there also, for the co-operative movement.

And the ultimate aim? Well, that just remains an ultimate aim. " The working classes have no fixed and perfect Utopias to introduce by means of a vote of the nation. They know that in order to work out their own emancipation—and with it that higher form of life which the present form of society irresistibly makes for by its own economic development—they, the working classes, have to pass through long struggles, a whole series of historical processes, by means of which men and circumstances will be completely transformed. They have no ideals to realise, they have only to set at liberty the elements of the new society which have already been developed in the womb of the collapsing bourgeois society." So writes Marx in *Civil War in France*. I was thinking of this utterance, not in every point, but in its fundamental thought in writing down the sentence about the ultimate aim. For after all what does it say but that the movement, the series of processes, is everything, whilst every aim fixed beforehand in its details is immaterial to it. I have declared already that I willingly abandon the form of the sentence about the ultimate aim as far as it admits the interpretation that every general aim of the working class movement formulated as a principle should be declared valueless. But the preconceived theories about the drift of the movement which go beyond such a generally expressed aim, which try to determine the

direction of the movement and its character
without an ever-vigilant eye upon facts and
experience, must necessarily always pass into
Utopianism, and at some time or other stand in
the way, and hinder the real theoretical and
practical progress of the movement.

Whoever knows even but a little of the
history of German social democracy also knows
that the party has become important by continued action in contravention of such theories
and of infringing resolutions founded on them.
What Engels says in the preface to the new
edition of *Civil War* with regard to the Blanquists and Proudhonists in the Paris Commune
of 1871, namely that they both had been
obliged in practice to act against their own
theory, has often been repeated in another form.
A theory or declaration of principle which does
not allow attention being paid at every stage of
development to the actual interests of the
working classes, will always be set aside just
as all foreswearing of reforming detail work
and of the support of neighbouring middle class
parties has again and again been forgotten;
and again and again at the congresses of the
party will the complaint be heard that here and
there in the electoral contest the ultimate aim of
socialism has not been put sufficiently in the
foreground.

In the quotation from Schulze-Gävernitz
which Plechanow flings at me, it runs that by
giving up the dictum that the condition of the
worker in modern society is hopeless, socialism
would lose its revolutionary point and would

be absorbed in carrying out legislative demands. From this contrast it is clearly inferred that Schulze-Gävernitz always used the concept " revolutionary " in the sense of a struggle having revolution by violence in view. Plechanow turns the thing round, and because I have not maintained the condition of the worker to be hopeless, because I acknowledge its capability of improvement and many other facts which bourgeois economists have upheld, he carts me over to the "opponents of scientific socialism."

Unfortunately for the scientific socialism of Plechanow, the Marxist propositions on the hopelessness of the position of the worker have been upset in a book which bears the title, *Capital: A Criticism of Political Economy.* There we read of the " physical and moral regeneration " of the textile workers in Lancashire through the Factory Law of 1847, which " struck the feeblest eye." A bourgeois republic was not even necessary to bring about a certain improvement in the situation of a large section of workers ! In the same book we read that the society of to-day is no firm crystal, but an organism capable of change and constantly engaged in a process of change, that also in the treatment of economic questions on the part of the official representatives of this society an " improvement was unmistakable." Further that the author had devoted so large a space in his book to the results of the English Factory Laws in order to spur the Continent to imitate them and thus to work so that the process of transforming society may be accomplished in ever more humane forms.* All of which signifies not hopelessness but capability of improvement in the condition of the worker. And, as since 1866, when this was written, the legislation depicted has not grown weaker but has been improved, made more general, and has been supplemented by laws and organisations working in the same direction, there can be no more doubt to-day than formerly of the hopefulness of the position of the worker. If to state such facts means following the " immortal Bastiat," then among the first ranks of these followers is—Karl Marx.

Now, it can be asserted against me that Marx certainly recognised those improvements, but that the chapter on the historical tendency of capitalist accumulation at the end of the first volume of *Capital* shows how little these details influenced his fundamental mode of viewing things. To which I answer that as far as that is correct it speaks against that chapter and not against me.

One can interpret this chapter in very different kinds of ways. I believe I was the first to point out, and indeed repeatedly, that it was a summary characterisation of the tendency of a development which is found in capitalist accumulation, but which in practice is not carried out completely and which therefore need not be driven to the critical point of the antagonism there depicted. Engels has

---

* Preface.

never expressed himself against this interpretation of mine, never, either verbally or in print, declared it to be wrong. Nor did he say a word against me when I wrote, in 1891, in an essay on a work of Schulze-Gävernitz on the questions referred to : "It is clear that where legislation, this systematic and conscious action of society, interferes in an appropriate way, the working of the tendencies of economic development is thwarted, under some circumstances can even be annihilated. Marx and Engels have not only never denied this, but, on the contrary, have always emphasised it."* If one reads the chapter mentioned with this idea, one will also, in a few sentences, silently place the word "tendency" and thus be spared the need of bringing this chapter into accord with reality by distorting arts of interpretation. But then the chapter itself would become of less value the more progress is made in actual evolution. For its theoretic importance does not lie in the argument of the general tendency to capitalistic centralisation and accumulation which had been affirmed long before Marx by bourgeois economists and socialists, but in the presentation, peculiar to Marx, of circumstances and forms under which it would work at a more advanced stage of evolution, and of the results to which it would lead. But in this respect actual evolution is really always bringing forth new arrangements, forces, facts, in face of which that presentation seems insufficient and loses to a corresponding

---

* *Neue Zeit* ix., 1, p. 736.

extent the capability of serving as a sketch of
the coming evolution. That is how I understand it.

One can, however, understand this chapter
differently. One can conceive it in this way,
that all the improvements mentioned there, and
some possibly ensuing, only create temporary
remedies against the oppressive tendencies of
capitalism, that they signify unimportant
modifications which cannot in the long run
effect anything substantially against the critical
point of antagonisms laid down by Marx, that
this will finally appear—if not literally yet
substantially—in the manner depicted, and will
lead to catastrophic change by violence. This
interpretation can be founded on the categoric
wording of the last sentences of the chapter,
and receives a certain confirmation because at
the end reference is again made to the *Communist Manifesto,* whilst Hegel also appeared
shortly before with his negation of the negation—the restoration on a new foundation of
individual property negatived by the capitalist
manner of production.

According to my view, it is impossible
simply to declare the one conception right and
the other absolutely wrong. To me the chapter
illustrates a dualism which runs through the
whole monumental work of Marx, and which
also finds expression in a less pregnant fashion
in other passages—a dualism which consists
in this, that the work aims at being a scientific
inquiry and also at proving a theory laid down
long before its drafting; a formula lies at the

basis of it in which the result to which the exposition should lead is fixed beforehand. The return to the *Communist Manifesto* points here to a real residue of Utopianism in the Marxist system. Marx had accepted the solution of the Utopians in essentials, but had recognised their means and proofs as inadequate. He therefore undertook a revision of them, and this with the zeal, the critical acuteness, and love of truth of a scientific genius. He suppressed no important fact, he also forebore belittling artificially the importance of these facts as long as the object of the inquiry had no immediate reference to the final aim of the formula to be proved. To that point his work is free of every tendency necessarily interfering with the scientific method.*

For the general sympathy with the strivings for emancipation of the working classes does not in itself stand in the way of the scientific method. But, as Marx approaches a point when that final aim enters seriously into the question, he becomes uncertain and unreliable. Such contradictions then appear as were shown in the book under consideration, for instance, in the section on the movement of incomes in modern society. It thus appears that this great scientific spirit was, in the end, a slave to a doctrine. To express it figuratively, he has raised a mighty building within the

* I take no account of that tendency which finds expression in the treatment of persons and the representation of occurrences, and which has no necessary connection with the analysis of the economic evolution.

framework of a scaffolding he found existing,
and in its erection he kept strictly to the laws of
scientific architecture as long as they did not
collide with the conditions which the construc-
tion of the scaffolding prescribed, but he
neglected or evaded them when the scaffolding
did not allow of their observance. Where the
scaffolding put limits in the way of the building,
instead of destroying the scaffolding, he changed
the building itself at the cost of its right proportions and so made it all the more dependent
on the scaffolding. Was it the consciousness
of this irrational relation which caused him
continually to pass from completing his work
to amending special parts of it ? However that may be, my conviction is that
wherever that dualism shows itself the scaffolding must fall if the building is to grow in
its right proportions. In the latter, and not
in the former, is found what is worthy to live
in Marx.

Nothing confirms me more in this conception
than the anxiety with which some persons seek
to maintain certain statements in *Capital,*
which are falsified by facts. It is just some of
the more deeply devoted followers of Marx
who have not been able to separate themselves
from the dialectical form of the work—that is
the scaffolding alluded to—who do this. At
least, that is only how I can explain the words
of a man, otherwise so amenable to facts as
Kautsky, who, when I observed in Stuttgart
that the number of wealthy people for many
years had increased, not decreased, answered :

" If that were true then the date of our victory would not only be very long postponed, but we should never attain our goal. If it be capitalists who increase and not those with no possessions, then we are going ever further from our goal the more evolution progresses, then capitalism grows stronger, not socialism."

That the number of the wealthy increases and does not diminish is not an invention of bourgeois "harmony economists," but a fact established by the boards of assessment for taxes, often to the chagrin of those concerned, a fact which can no longer be disputed. But what is the significance of this fact as regards the victory of socialism? Why should the realisation of socialism depend on its refutation? Well, simply for this reason : because the dialectical scheme seems so to prescribe it; because a post threatens to fall out of the scaffolding if one admits that the social surplus product is appropriated by an increasing instead of a decreasing number of possessors. But it is only the speculative theory that is affected by this matter; it does not at all affect the actual movement. Neither the struggle of the workers for democracy in politics nor their struggle for democracy in industry is touched by it. The prospects of this struggle do not depend on the theory of concentration of capital in the hands of a diminishing number of magnates, nor on the whole dialectical scaffolding of which this is a plank, but on the growth of social wealth and of the social productive forces, in conjunction with general social progress, and, particularly, in conjunction with the intellectual and moral advance of the working classes themselves.

Suppose the victory of socialism depended on the constant shrinkage in the number of capitalist magnates, social democracy, if it wanted to act logically, either would have to support the heaping up of capital in ever fewer hands, or at least to give no support to anything that would stop this shrinkage. As a matter of fact it often enough does neither the one nor the other. These considerations, for instance, do not govern its votes on questions of taxation. From the standpoint of the catastrophic theory a great part of this practical activity of the working classes is an undoing of work that ought to be allowed to be done. It is not social democracy which is wrong in this respect. The fault lies in the doctrine which assumes that progress depends on the deterioration of social conditions.

In his preface to the *Agrarian Question,* Kautsky turns upon those who speak of the necessity of a triumph over Marxism. He says that he sees doubt and hesitation expressed, but that these alone indicate no development. That is so far correct in that doubt and hesitation are no positive refutation. They can, however, be the first step towards it. But is it altogether a matter of triumphing over Marxism, or is it not rather a rejection of certain remains of Utopianism which adhere to Marxism, and which are the cause of the contradictions in theory and practice which have been pointed out in Marxism by its critics? This treatise has become already more voluminous than it ought to have been, and I must therefore abstain from going into all the details of this subject. But all the more I consider it my duty to declare that I hold a whole series of objections raised by opponents against certain items in Marx's theory as unrefuted, some as irrefutable. And I can do this all the more easily as these objections are quite irrelevant to the strivings of social democracy.

We ought to be less susceptible in this respect. It has repeatedly happened that conclusions by followers of Marx, who believed that they contradicted the theories of Marx, have been disputed with great zeal, and, in the end, the supposed contradictions were proved for the most part not to exist. Amongst others I have in my mind the controversy concerning the investigations of the late Dr. Stiebling on the effect of the concentration of capital on the rate of exploitation. In his manner of expression, as well as in separate items of his calculations, Stiebling made some great blunders, which it is the merit of Kautsky to have discovered. But on the other hand the third volume of *Capital* has shown that the fundamental thought of Stiebling's works—the decrease of the rate of exploitation with the increasing concentration of capital did not stand in such opposition to Marx's doctrine as then appeared to most of us, although his proof of the phenomenon is different from that of Marx. Yet in his time Stiebling had to hear (from

Kautsky) that if what he inferred was correct, the theoretical foundation of the working class movement, the theory of Marx, was false. And as a matter of fact those who spoke thus could refer to various passages from Marx. An analysis of the controversy which was entered into over the essays of Stiebling could very well serve as an illustration of some of the contradictions of the Marxist theory of value.

Similar conflicts exist with regard to the estimate of the relation of economics and force in history, and they find their counterpart in the criticism on the practical tasks and possibilities of the working class movement which has already been discussed in another place. This is, however, a point to which it is necessary to recur. But the question to be investigated is not how far originally, and in the further course of history, force determined economy and *vice versa,* but what is the creative power of force in a given society.

Now it would be absurd to go back to the prejudices of former generations with regard to the capabilities of political power, for such a thing would mean that we would have to go still further back to explain those prejudices. The prejudices which the Utopians, for example, cherished rested on good grounds; indeed, one can scarcely say that they were prejudices, for they rested on the real immaturity of the working classes of the period as a result of which, only a transitory mob rule on the one side or a return to the class oligarchy on the other was the only possible outcome of the political power of the masses. Under these circumstances a reference to politics could appear only to be a turning aside from more pressing duties. To-day these conditions have been to some extent removed, and therefore no person capable of reflecting will think of criticising political action with the arguments of that period.

Marxism first turned the thing round, as we have seen, and preached (in view of the potential capacity of the industrial proletariat) political action as the most important duty of the movement. But it was thereby involved in great contradictions. It also recognised, and separated itself thereby from the demagogic parties, that the working classes had not yet attained the required maturity for their emancipation, and also that the economic preliminary conditions for such were not present. But in spite of that it turned again and again to tactics which supposed both preliminary conditions as almost fulfilled. We come across passages in its publications where the immaturity of the workers is emphasised with an acuteness which differs very little from the doctrinairism of the early Utopian socialists, and soon afterwards we come across passages according to which we should assume that all culture, all intelligence, all virtue, is only to be found among the working classes—passages which make it incomprehensible why the most extreme social revolutionaries and physical force anarchists should not be right.

Corresponding with that, political action is ever directed towards a revolutionary convulsion expected in an imminent future, in the face of which legislative work for a long time appears only as a *pis aller*—a merely temporary device. And we look in vain for any systematic investigation of the question of what can be expected from legal, and what from revolutionary action.

It is evident at the first glance that great differences exist in the latter respect. But they are usually found to be this : that law, or the path of legislative reform, is the slower way, and revolutionary force the quicker and more radical.* But that only is true in a restricted sense. Whether the legislative or the revolutionary method is the more promising depends entirely on the nature of the measures and on their relation to different classes and customs of the people.

In general, one may say here that the revolutionary way (always in the sense of revolution by violence) does quicker work as far as it deals with removal of obstacles which a privileged minority places in the path of social progress : that its strength lies on its negative side.

Constitutional legislation works more slowly

---

* In this sense Marx speaks in *Capital,* in the chapter about the working day, of the " peculiar advantages of the French revolutionary method " which had been made manifest in the French twelve hours' law of 1848. It dictates for all workers and all factories without distinction the same working day. That is right. But it has been ascertained that this radical law remained a dead letter for a whole generation.

in this respect as a rule. Its path is usually that of compromise, not the prohibition, but the buying out of acquired rights. But it is stronger than the revolution scheme where prejudice and the limited horizon of the great mass of the people appear as hindrances to social progress, and it offers greater advantages where it is a question of the creation of permanent economic arrangements capable of lasting; in other words, it is best adapted to positive social-political work.

In legislation, intellect dominates over emotion in quiet times; during a revolution emotion dominates over intellect. But if emotion is often an imperfect leader, the intellect is a slow motive force. Where a revolution sins by over haste, the every-day legislator sins by procrastination. Legislation works as a systematic force, revolution as an elementary force.

As soon as a nation has attained a position where the rights of the propertied minority have ceased to be a serious obstacle to social progress, where the negative tasks of political action are less pressing than the positive, then the appeal to a revolution by force becomes a meaningless phrase.* One can overturn a government or a privileged minority, but not a nation. When the working classes do not possess very strong economic organisations of their own, and have not attained,

---

* "Fortunately, 'revolution' in this country has ceased to be anything more than an affected phrase."—The monthly *News* of the Independent Labour Party in England, Jan., 1899.

by means of education on self-governing
bodies, a high degree of mental independence,
the dictatorship of the proletariat means
the dictatorship of club orators and writers.
I would not wish that those who see in the
oppression and tricking of the working men's
organisations and in the exclusion of working
men from the legislature and government the
highest point of the art of political policy should
experience their error in practice. Just as
little would I desire it for the working class
movement itself.

One has not overcome Utopianism if one
assumes that there is in the present, or ascribes
to the present, what is to be in the future.
We have to take working men as they are.
And they are neither so universally pauperised
as was set out in the *Communist Manifesto,*
nor so free from prejudices and weaknesses as
their courtiers wish to make us believe. They
have the virtues and failings of the economic
and social conditions under which they live.
And neither these conditions nor their effects
can be put on one side from one day to another.

Have we attained the required degree of
development of the productive forces for the
abolition of classes? In face of the fantastic
figures which were formerly set up in proof of
this and which rested on generalisations based
on the development of particularly favoured
industries, socialist writers in modern times
have endeavoured to reach by carefully detailed
calculations, appropriate estimates of the
possibilities of production in a socialist society,

and their results are very different from those figures.* Of a general reduction of hours of labour to five, four, or even three or two hours, such as was formerly accepted, there can be no hope at any time within sight, unless the general standard of life is much reduced. Even under a collective organisation of work, labour must begin very young and only cease at a rather advanced age, it is to be reduced considerably below an eight-hours' day. Those persons ought to understand this first of all who indulge in the most extreme exaggerations regarding the ratio of the number of the non-propertied classes to that of the propertied. But he who thinks irrationally on one point does so usually on another. And, therefore, I am not surprised if the same Plechanow, who is angered to see the position of working men represented as not hopeless, has only the annihilating verdict, " Philistine," for my conclusions on the impossibility at any period within sight of abandoning the principle of the economic self-responsibility of those capable of working. It is not for nothing that one is the philosopher of irresponsibility.

---

* Compare Atlanticus : *A Glance into the State of the Future : Production and consumption in the Social State* (Stuttgart : Dietz), as well as the Essays : *Something on Collectivism*, by Dr. Joseph Ritter von Neupauer in Pernerstorfer's *Deutsche Worte* for 1897-98. These works are not free from objection, but they are to be warmly recommended to those who wish to learn about the problems referred to. Neupauer thinks that if the average work done by all machines were reckoned it would be shown that they barely save a third of human labour power.

But he who surveys the actual workers' movement will also find that the freedom from those qualities which appeared Philistine to a person born in the bourgeoisie, is very little valued by the workers, that they in no way support the morale of proletarianism, but, on the contrary, tend to make a " Philistine " out of a proletarian. With the roving proletarian without a family and home, no lasting, firm trade union movement would be possible. It is no bourgeois prejudice, but a conviction gained through decades of labour organisation, which has made so many of the English labour leaders—socialists and non-socialists—into zealous adherents of the temperance movement. The working class socialists know the faults of their class, and the most conscientious among them, far from glorifying these faults, seek to overcome them with all their power.

We cannot demand from a class, the great majority of whose members live under crowded conditions, are badly educated, and have an uncertain and insufficient income, the high intellectual and moral standard which the organisation and existence of a socialist community presupposes. We will, therefore, not ascribe it to them by way of fiction. Let us rejoice at the great stock of intelligence, renunciation, and energy which the modern working class movement has partly revealed, partly produced; but we must not assign, without discrimination to the masses, the millions, what holds good, say, of hundreds of thousands. I will not repeat the declarations which have been made to me on this point by working men verbally and in writing; I do not need to defend myself before reasonable persons against the suspicion of Pharisaism and the conceit of pedantry. But I confess willingly that I measure here with two kinds of measures. Just because I expect much of the working classes I censure much more everything that tends to corrupt their moral judgment than I do similar habits of the higher classes, and I see with the greatest regret that a tone of literary decadence is spreading here and there in the working class press which can only have a confusing and corrupting effect. A class which is aspiring needs a sound morale and must suffer no deterioration. Whether it sets out for itself an ideal ultimate aim is of secondary importance if it pursues with energy its proximate aims. The important point is that these aims are inspired by a definite principle which expresses a higher degree of economy and of social life, that they are an embodiment of a social conception which means in the evolution of civilisation a higher view of morals and of legal rights.

From this point of view I cannot subscribe to the proposition: "The working class has no ideas to realise." I see in it rather a self-deception, if it is not a mere play upon words on the part of its author.

And in this mind, I, at the time, resorted to the spirit of the great Königsberg philosopher, the critic of pure reason, against the cant which sought to get a hold on the working class movement and to which the Hegelian dialetic offers a comfortable refuge. I did this in the conviction that social democracy required a Kant who should judge the received opinion and examine it critically with deep acuteness, who should show where its apparent materialism is the highest—and is therefore the most easily misleading—ideology, and warn it that the contempt of the ideal, the magnifying of material factors until they become omnipotent forces of evolution, is a self-deception, which has been and will be exposed as such at every opportunity by the action of those who proclaim it. Such a thinker, who with convincing exactness could show what is worthy and destined to live in the work of our great champions, and what must and can perish, would also make it possible for us to hold a more unbiassed judgment on those works which, although not starting from premises which to-day appear to us as decisive, yet are devoted to the ends for which social democracy is fighting. No impartial thinker will deny that socialist criticism often fails in this and discloses all the dark sides of epigonism. I have myself done my share in this, and therefore cast a stone at no one. But just because I belong to the school, I believe I am justified in giving expression to the need for reform. If I did not fear that what I write should be misunderstood (I am, of course, prepared for its being misconstrued), I would translate *Back to Kant* by *Back to Lange.* For, just as the philosophers and investigators who stand by that motto are not concerned

with going back to the letter of what the
Königsberg philosopher wrote, but are only
concerned with the fundamental principles of
his criticism, so social democracy would just as
little think of going back to all the social-
political views of Frederick Albert Lange.
What I have in mind is the distinguishing
union in Lange of an upright and intrepid
championship of the struggles of the working
classes for emancipation with a large scientific
freedom from prejudice which was always
ready to acknowledge mistakes and recognise
new truths. Perhaps such a great broad-
mindedness as meets us in Lange's writings is
only to be found in persons who are wanting
in the penetrating acuteness which is the property of pioneer spirits like Marx. But it is
not every epoch that produces a Marx, and
even for a man of equal genius the working
class movement of to-day is too great to enable
him to occupy the position which Marx fills in
its history. To-day it needs, in addition to the
fighting spirit, the co-ordinating and construc-
tive thinkers who are intellectually enough
advanced to be able to separate the chaff from
the wheat, who are great enough in their mode
of thinking to recognise also the little plant
that has grown on another soil than theirs, and
who, perhaps, though not kings, are warm-
hearted republicans in the domain of socialist
thought.